Get That Cutie in Commercials, Television, Films, and Videos

Breaking Your Talented Child into the Entertainment Industry

The African-American Parents Step-by-Step
Beginner's Guide to Show Business Success

By Kandias Conda

Amber Books
Los Angeles, CA   Phoenix, AZ

Get That Cutie in Commercials, Television, Films, and Videos / Breaking Your Talented Child into the Entertainment Industry The African-American Parents Step-by-Step Beginner's Guide to Show Business Success

by Kandias Conda

Published by:
AMBER BOOKS
1334 East Chandler Boulevard. Suite 5-D67 Phoenix. AZ 85048
Email: amberbk@aol.com
www.amberbooks.com

The publication is designed to provide accurate and authoritative information in regard to the subject matter covered. It is sold with the understanding that the Publisher is not engaged in rendering legal, accounting or other professional services. If legal advice or other expert assistance is required, the services of a competent professional person should be sought.

AMBER BOOKS are available at special discounts for bulk purchases, sales promotions, fund raising or educational purposes. For details contact: Special Sales Department, AMBER BOOKS, 1334 East Chandler Boulevard, Suite 5-D67, Phoenix, AZ 85048, USA.

Copyright 2001 by Kandias Conda and AMBER BOOKS
ISBN #: 0-9655064-5-2

Library of Congress Cataloging-In-Publication Data

Conda, Kandias.
  "Get that cutie in commercials, television, films and videos": breaking your talented
  child into the entertainment industry: the African-American parents step-by-step
  beginner's handbook and guide to show business success / by Kandias Conda.
      p. cm
  ISBN 0-9655064-5-2 (alk. Paper)
  1. Performing arts--Vocational guidance--United States. 2. Child actors--United States.
  3. African-American--United States. I. Title.

PN1580.C64 1998
792'.028'02373--dc21
                                                                              98-045571

January 2001
10 9 8 7 6 5 4 3 2 1

Contents

Dedication

I'd like to dedicate this book to my mother Selma Sewell, who edited my original manuscript. I wish she was here to see it come to fruition, but I know her hand of spirit has touched the entire book throughout, and I know she is watching over this book. I also dedicate this book to my daughter, who was the motivating inspirational force behind me writing this book.

Acknowledgments

First and foremost, I thank God for making this all possible. I'd like to thank Tony Rose of Amber Books for his vision of educating women, children and their families in his publishing efforts. I'd also like to thank Tony Rose for being patient and believing in this project. To my daughter Deminique and all of the people who let us interview them. To my friends and family, Theresa Conda-Miller, Patrice Conda, and Donna Beasley who believed in and supported me. Thanks to Rochelle McCall, Priscilla Paris-Austin, Nambi and all other interviewees.

I'd also like to thank Sa'Rah Talent Agency, Stewart Talent Agency, and McCall Talent Agencies for participating in our seminars for parents and children. A special thanks goes out to Caletha, Corey & Jared White for attending our entertainment seminars and sharing their information with aspiring entertainment families and their children. A very special thanks to Jefferey Radford of Trinity United Church of Christ for also lending his musical expertise to our panel for our aspiring musicians. To moms and dads of entertainers everywhere—keep your children and their careers close to you at all times. It's not just a hobby it's an investment of your time, your love and your money.

A Special Acknowledgment:

Tony Rose, Publisher and Editorial Director
Samuel P. Peabody, Associate Publisher
Yvonne Rose, Associate Editor
Joe Liddy, Proofreader
Lisa Liddy, Cover and Interior Design
Wayne Parham, Cover and Interior Photographs
Pamela Young, Models Plus International
Alnisia Cruz, Natori's Club, Children's Talent Agency
Natori's Club Child Models: Natori Ja'nez, Tiara,
Iris Yoery, Charles C. Henry, and Monique
Child Models: Jonathon Beams, JoAnn E. Davis,
Sullivan Stallworth III, Tyreik S. Stallworth, Brie' Harriel,
Roshann Hooks, Gianna Jordan, Tienna M. White,
Michael Price, Jaques Philippe Rene, Zariyah Necoye,
Christopher Applewhite, Yvonne Fleetwood, Keith Carroll,
Joann Herbert, Gabrielle Fleetwood, Brandon Butler, Jade Butler,
and Jazmin Butler
Photographers: Tony Barboza, James Davis, James Thaxton, Wai Ng
For Natori's Club Children Models

As always the Publisher gratefully acknowledges those whose time, patience, help, and advice have contributed to the success of our literary efforts:

Erline Belton; Philip and Anjie Herbert; Felicia Rose and Kate Saylor; Florence Price; Regina Thomas; Elnora Marie Fleetwood-Miles; Yvonne Marie Fleetwood; Lloyd and Lamurel King; Kevin Anthony Fleetwood, Jr.; John and Mildred Seagraves; Kay Bourne; Cassandra Latney; Therese Fleetwood; Jamila White; Wayne Summerlin; Lisa Liddy; Rodney J. McKissic; Alfred Fornay; Carolyn Herbert; Tom "Satch" Sanders; Samuel P. Peabody; Darryl and Lorraine Sanders; Mrs. Muriel Waller; Mack Lee; Terri Simmons, PhD.; Terrie Williams, Kendal and Revola Minter, Yvonne Rose; Donna Beasley, founder of the Chicago Black Book Fair and Conference; the IBBMEC; the Nation's African-American bookstores; our wholesalers and distributors; the black media; and to Kandias Conda for writing a truly remarkable and informative book.

Deminique E. Lobo

Foreword

Several years ago, I was talking with a group of other moms, trying to figure out the secret to getting our "yet to be discovered" talented offspring in commercials. Chicago is a very competitive area for the commercial market, so I began Annual Entertainment Symposiums (AES) to bring parents and their children face to face with the powers that be—major well-known agents, producers, and casting directors. We also bring in photographers and stage moms along with their TV children to share their expertise directly with parents. This gives unique and in depth insight to aspiring parents of cute, talented, bubbly babies, toddlers and children with personality plus. AES was created to give parents first hand knowledge of the industry and provide them opportunities to meet with professionals in person. I am in the business of helping others make "their dream happen."

My daughter is not a Broadway star, she still doesn't have a cereal box...not yet. But what she does have is a rounded entertainment career that entails several different areas. That's what this book is all about. I'm a regular mom, just like you. Matter of a fact, while in the midst of writing this book—just when I thought my daughter was on the verge of her big break, she decided to take a break from it all. She wanted to further her gift of song. I'm like "oh man...are you sure?" I gave a big sigh, took a deep breath and said "Well OK, I guess so." I was a little disappointed, but after all, who's life is this anyway. I researched this book to help others—especially the

Introduction

Children are in commercials selling everything—Pampers, McDonald's hamburgers, baby shampoo, clothing, and cars. Just turn on the television, open up a newspaper or magazine, they're everywhere. If you're like me you've probably said to yourself, "I know my child can do that!"

Many parents are not quite sure if they are ready for the entertainment industry. Some have heard negative stories in the press, and some parents just do not have the time. The truth of the matter is...if you've got an adorable baby, cute toddler, or personality plus kid – then you should seriously consider "getting that cutie in commercials." It's not impossible or as hard as you think. Your child may be the next Jonathan Taylor Thomas, Brandy, Mary Kate and Ashley or the cutest little baby that ever wore a diaper on television.

If your child frequently asks you to get them in the business, talk of becoming an actor, is very outgoing, smiley, bubbly, performs in front of family without coaxing, or doesn't cry easily when separated from you, then you should get that cutie in commercials, print, film, television, or video.

Children of all ethnicities, ages, sizes, and shapes appear in commercials. Regardless of physical disabilities, looks, or experience your child can be in commercials, film, television, videos and magazines. We're going to show you just how to do it!!!

Famous Child Stars
Past and Present

From Janet Jackson's adorable face in Good Times to Drew Barrymore in ET, these are the children's faces that are implanted in our childhood thoughts when we think of children actors. Remember the famous faces of the forties – Mickey Rooney and Shirley Temple? McCauley Culkin, Kim Fields, and Gary Coleman, are just a few from the 70's and 80's. As we come to the new age WB network we have such positive role models as Tia & Tamera Mowry on *Sister Sister*, their adorable brother Tahj Mowry on *Smart Guy*, Jason Weaver who has had starring roles on *Smart Guy* and Thea, Brandy (what a winner!) and the list goes on and on. Ron Howard grew up as Opie on *The Andy Griffith Show*, and has become the awe of most child stars as he's made an impressive transition from child actor to directing for major television and film.

Hollywood has been both great and nostalgic, but also tragic to some of these stars. We have watched the rise and fall and personal tabloid trials of Todd Bridges, Gary Coleman and McCauley Culkin. We have also watched the bright and promising family managed, family oriented career of Brandy Norwood.

The entertainment business can be a wonderful experience. Keep expectations moderate. Be grateful for the blessings that come your way. Stay educated in your child's area. And, keep an entourage of friends and family for support.

Now, read about those child stars who have made it through perseverance and hard work.

Celebrity Biographies

TATYANA ALI

Singer & Actress – Born January 24, 1979 – Brooklyn, New York
This talented young lady has been performing since she was 4 years old. At age 7, Tatyana starred in *Fences*. When she was 11 years old, Tatyana landed her role as Will Smith's young cousin on *Fresh Prince of Bel Air* – a role which lasted from 1990 until 1996. During that time, she continued to star in other television shows and she branched into feature films. Among Tatyana's credits are such television shows as *413 Hope Street, Living Single*, and *In the House*; and films such as *Crocodile Dundee II, Fall into Darkness* and *Kiss the Girls*. Tatyana's musical career was launched when she sang on an episode of *Fresh Prince of Bel Air*. Will Smith signed her to his Will Smith Entertainment Production Company, took her into the recording studio, made a demo tape and got her a contract with MJJ Music. Tatyana's hits include *Kiss The Sky, Day Dreamin, Boy You Knock Me Out* and *Everytime*.

DEBBIE ALLEN

Dancer, Singer, Actress, Television Producer, Writer, Director – Born January 16, 1950
At age 3 Debbie began her dance training. By age 8, having been inspired by a performance of *Revelations* by Alvin Ailey, she had settled on a future in musical theater. Her mother, who she considered her mentor was an active participant in her training. Among the many lessons she provided, she contracted the Ballett Russe to give her daughter private lessons. In addition to her fame as a dancer, Debbie has starred on Broadway as Purlie in *Purlie Victorious*, she has been in *Raisin* and she was nominated for a Tony for her role in *West Side Story*. Among her numerous television credits are included *Fame, A Different World* and *In The House*.

HALLE BERRY

Actress – Born August 14, 1966 – Cleveland, Ohio
With a white mother and a black father, Halle grew up taunted by the kids in school. She became determined to fit in and excelled in everything she did as a cheerleader, honor society member, school paper editor, class president and prom queen. As her life's quest continued, she was crowned Miss Teen Ohio and competed in Miss Teen All-American, Miss USA and Miss World. Halle parlayed her many experiences into a successful modeling career and then turned to acting. She has starred in numerous films, including: *X-Men, Introducing Dorothy Dandridge, Bulworth* and *Why Do Fools Fall in Love?*. *People* magazine voted Halle Berry one of the 50 Most Beautiful People of 1998. In September 2000, she won an Emmy award for "Best Actress in a Made for TV Drama" for her starring role in *Introducing Dorothy Dandridge*.

BRANDY

Singer, Actress, Musician, Model – Born February 11, 1979 – McComb, Missouri
Her father was a church music director and Brandy started singing in the church choir at an early age. In 1994 when she was just 15 years old, her hit album *Brandy* sold over 4 million copies. After its release, she took a break to establish an acting career and starred in her own television show *Moesha* and in other shows, such as: *Double Platinum* and *Cinderella*, and the film *I Still Know What You Did Last Summer*. Brandy has won numerous awards, including: 1995 MTV Movie Award for Best Song *Sittin Up in My Room*. 1996 NAACP Image Award for Best New Artist, 1997 NAACP Image Award for Best Youth Actor/Actress, 1999 Grammy for This Boy is Mine. She recently, swung back into music with her follow-up hit *Never Say Never* and is continuing her education at Pepperdine University in Malibu, California.

TODD BRIDGES

Actor, Producer, Director, Cinematographer, Writer – Born May 27, 1965 – San Francisco, California
By age 13, Todd landed the part of Willis Jackson in the television sitcom *Different Strokes*. His many roles that kept him in show business include, *Katherine* (at age 10), *Roots* (at age 12), *Return of Mod Squad* (at age 14) and the list goes on. As an offshoot of his acting career, Todd began to produce and direct films. Included in those credits are *Black Ball* and *Flossin*.

GARY COLEMAN

Actor – Born February 8, 1968 – Zion, Illinois
At the age of 10, Gary Coleman was a household name. He played the loveable Arnold Jackson in the television sitcom Different Strokes. He went on to star in a multitude of films, including: *Jimmy the Kid, Like Father, Like Santa, Scout's Honor, Kid in the Broken Halo* and appeared on such television sitcoms as: *Good Times, The Jeffersons, Facts of Life, Silver Spoons* and *Cheers*, to name a few.

CHRISTINA AGUILERA

Singer – Born December 18, 1980 – Staten Island, New York
Christina was always performing. When she was 8 years old, she appeared on *Star Search*. When she was 10 years old, she sang the National Anthem for the Pittsburgh Steelers and the Penguins. When she was 12 years old Christina became a Mousketeer on the *Mickey Mouse Club*. Fate knocked on her door the day she sang in her living room and recorded the demo for a movie score on a boombox. Days later, Christina's career was launched when she sang that same song *Reflection* for the animated movie *Mulan*. All the world loves to watch Christina in the videos *Genie in a Bottle* and *What a Girl Wants*, but even though she has been approached to act, she prefers to focus on her music right now.

DREW BARRYMORE

Actress – Born February 22, 1975 – Los Angeles, CA
Drew has starred in many films including, *Never Been Kissed, Ever After, The Wedding Singer, Scream, Firestarter, Home, Fries, Mad Love* and *ET* which launched her acting career. After the success of *ET*, Drew began drinking and taking drugs and found herself in rehab at the tender age of 13. The experience helped her to deal with life, as she revealed in an interview "It wasn't about being sober and cleaning up. It was about learning to live." Drew comes from a long line of show business royalty, including her grandfather John Barrymore and her uncle, Lionel Barrymore; and Steven Spielberg is her Godfather.

OMAR EPPS

Actor – Born May 16, 1973 – Brooklyn, New York
Omar didn't initially plan to go into acting. In college he majored in engineering, but he had had a taste of fame when he was part of the rap group called Da Wolfpack and directed music videos for Heath B and Special Ed. Having revealed a natural talent, he drifted into acting and has since landed numerous starring roles in films, such as *The Mod Squad, Scream II, Major League II* and on the television show *ER*.

KIM FIELDS

Actress and Director – Born May 12, 1969 – New York City
Being a child star in Hollywood had forced Kim to mature faster than conventional children – she had started wearing make-up steadily since the age of 10. Her mom, Chip Fields, who played the mother of Janet Jackson on *Good Times*, encouraged her to stay on track and to work hard. Kim's perseverance and professionalism acquired from several years of acting lessons and auditions eventually prevailed when, at age 13, she landed the role of Tootie (one of 4 girls enrolled in an expensive boarding school) on NBC's *Facts of Life*. Kim has appeared in several television shows, including *Different Strokes, Baby I'm Back, Roots-The Next Generation, Hollywood*

Squares, 227 and *Living Single.* Kim received her Bachelor's degree in Communications and film from Pepperdine University in an effort to expand her career. She has also directed numerous projects.

MC CAULAY CULKIN

Actor – Born August 26, 1980 – New York, New York

McCaulay has been acting all his life. He had his stage debut at age 4 in *Bach Babies.* He appeared on television in *The Equalizer* at age 5. His film credits began in 1988 when he was 8 years old with *Rocket Gibraltar*, in 1989 with *Uncle Buck*, From 1990 to 1994 his many film credits included *Home Alone, The Good Son, Home Alone 2, Pagemaster, Richie Rich* and *Getting Even With Dad.* By 1994, he was grossing $8 million a film.

LAWRENCE FISHBURNE

Actor – Born in 1962 in Augusta, Georgia

Lawrence Fishburne has spent his life acting. Included in his numerous and varied credits, he has starred in Cornbread, Earl & Me, Boyz in the Hood, Deep Cover, The Color Purple, Apocalypse Now, Othello, and the list goes on. Lawrence's father, who was a correction's officer, frequently took him to the movies. When the family moved to Brooklyn, New York Lawrence's mom, a teacher, introduced him to the theatre. He had his stage debut, at age 10, in *My Many Names* and *Days* at the Federal Theatre. Between the ages of 11 and 14, Lawrence was a regular on the television soap *One Life to Live.* In 1972, he starred in the television film *If You Give a Dance You've Got to Pay the Band.* The Negro Ensemble Theater Production member Lawrence Fishburne won a Tony in 1992 for the Broadway production *Two Trains Running.* As one of the world's most respected actors his credits are endless.

JASMINE GUY

Actress, dancer, singer – Born 1964 – Boston, MA

Jasmine sang regularly in the church choir, and at age 13 starred as Anita in West Side Story at Northside High School of Arts. At age 17, she went to New York to study dance with Alvin Ailey and later to Los Angeles as a dancer in the television show *Fame*. Additional credits include the television show *A Different World* and the Broadway show *Bubbling Brown Sugar*.

BRANDON HAMMOND

Actor – Born February 6, 1984

Brandon has appeared in several movies including *The Fan* and *Soul Food*. He has also co-starred in the sitcom *The Gregory Hines Show*. For his performance in *Soul Food*, Brandon received a NAACP Image Award. He has also appeared in *Waiting to Exhale*, *Mars Attacks*, *Space Jam* (as Michael Jordan), *Strange Days*, *Tales From the Hood, Road to Galveston*, and in 1993 at the age of 9, *Menace to Society*.

GREGORY HINDS

Actor & Dancer – Born February 14, 1946

Gregory started dancing when he was very young. When Gregory was 17 years old, his dad Maurice Hines Senior, formed the tap dance group Hinds, Hinds and Dad and they appeared on television shows such as *The Tonight Show* and *The Ed Sullivan Show*. Later Gregory turned his interests toward acting and starred in many television shows and films including: *White Nights* and *Running Scared*, and on Broadway in *Jelly's Last Jam*.

JANET JACKSON

Singer & Actress – Born 1966 – Gary, Indiana

Growing up in a musical family with her mother Katherine, her father Joe, her sister LaToya and her brothers Michael, Marlin, Tito, Jermaine and Jackie, Janet's interests branched out into dancing, acting and singing. She appeared on stage in her brothers – *The Jackson 5* – show at age 7. In 1977, when she was 11 years old, Norman Lear offered Janet a role as Penny Gordon Woods in *Good Times*. She later appeared in several sitcoms, such as: *Different Strokes* and *A New Kind of Family* and starred in the film *Poetic Justice*. In 1982, Janet's first album self-titled Janet was released, followed by *Dreamstreet* and in 1986 *Control*. Janet stepped out from the shadow of her famous musical brothers with this album. Since then Janet has recorded the hit albums *Rhythm Nation* and *The Velvet Rope*.

MICHAEL JACKSON

Singer, Songwriter, Producer – Born August 29, 1956 – Gary, Indiana

By the time he was 5 years old, Michael and his brothers Jackie, Tito, Jermaine and Marlon had formed an R & B act called the Jackson 5. Michael's dad, who was a musician, dedicated years to working with the group and they won their first talent competition in 1963, and in 1968 appeared at the world-famous Apollo Theater with the Temptations. In 1972, at the age of 16, Michael premiered as a solo artist. *Got to Be There*, which earned him a Grammy, was followed by the albums *Ben* and *Off the Wall*. Michael's next album *Thriller* went platinum in 15 countries, gold in 4 countries, and garnered 8 Grammies with sales exceeding 38 million copies worldwide. This feat landed him in the Guinness Book of World Records.

CHRISTOPHER KNIGHT

Actor – Born November 7, 1957
Christopher played Peter several seasons on *The Brady Bunch*. He has been in films since the age of 5 starring in *If A Man Answers*. Other credits include: *Diary of A Teenage Hitchhiker, Just You and Me Kid, Joe's World, Nowhere, Gunsmoke, Chips* and *The Bionic Woman*.

RON HOWARD

Actor & Director – Born March 1, 1954 – Duncan, Oklahoma
Ron's parents were theater actors. They moved to Hollywood when he was very young. At the age of 6, Ron got his first big acting role as Andy Griffith's son Opie Taylor on *The Andy Griffith Show*. He had already appeared on *Playhouse 90* and *The Red Skelton Show*. He also had recurring roles on *Dennis The Menace* and *The Many Loves of Dobie Gillis*. While he enjoyed acting, he was equally interested in filming and his parents gave him a movie camera to play around with. His acting career grew with various roles, primarily on television. He appeared in *Gentle Ben, The Smith Family* and really made it big as Richie Cunningham in *Happy Days*. After six years on the show, however, Ron left acting to pursue his dream as a director. Soon he was known as the best director in Hollywood. He has been nominated for and won numerous awards for directing films such as: *Apollo 13, Backdraft, Splash, Cocoon* and *Parenthood*.

EMMANUEL LEWIS

Actor – Born March 9, 1971 – Brooklyn, New York
When Emmanuel was five years old, he launched his acting career. He had been chosen over 150 other children for a Campbell's Soup ad. Thereafter, his mom kept him in the spotlight, attending audition after audition and was cast for many of the spots. An NBC executive caught the cute little kid's Burger King spot and immediately cast him as Webster. And the rest is history.

JENNIFER LOPEZ

Singer, Dancer and Actress – Born July 24, 1970 – Bronx, New York
As a little girl, Jennifer knew that she wanted to perform, so her parents put her into dance classes. She later beat out 2,000 other girls in a national dance contest and became one of Rosie Perez's Fly Girls on *In Living Color*. Jennifer's debut album *On the 6* has gone platinum. She has continued success as a sought after actress in films such as: *My Family, Mi Familia, The Cell* and *Out of Sight* and as a voice in *Antz*.

TREVOR MORGAN

Actor – Born November 26, 1986
Trevor had a recurring role in *ER* and can be seen in *Barney's Great Adventure*. He was nominated for a Young Artist Award as Best Performer in a TV Movie or Pilot for his role in *Genius*. In addition, Trevor starred in several films including: *The Sixth Sense, The Glass House, Patriot, Rumor of Angels* and on the television show *Touched by an Angel*.

HAYLEY MILLS

Actress – Born April 18, 1946 – London, England
Hayley's parents were actor John Mills and Playwright Mary Hayley Bell. She made her acting debut in the film *Tiger Bay* at the age of 13. The role was written for a boy, but when the director saw her by chance, he cast her on the spot. Although it was her first film, she did the scene in one take. Hayley was then discovered by Walt Disney's wife, when she saw her in the film. Thus she was cast in her first American film *Pollyanna*, for which she won a special Academy Award for her performance. Hayley then made history in *Parent Trap*. (While filming, she grew two inches and all 65 costumes had to be lengthened for her). Other films to Hayley's credit are: *A Matter of Innocense, The Chalk Garden, Endless Night, Deadly Stranger* and *Parent Trap: Hawaiian Honeymoon*.

JAKE LLOYD

Actor – Born March 5, 1989 – Fort Collins, CO
Jake had, at the age of 8, starred in *Jingle All The Way*. He has also been featured in *The Pretender, ER, Apollo 11, Virtual Obsession* and as Anakin Skywalker in *Star Wars Episode 1 - The Phantom Menace*. For this role he was nominated for a 1999 Hollywood Reporters Young Star Award as Best Young Actor/Performance in a Drama Film and won the 2000 Young Artist Award for Best Performance in a Feature Film – Young Actor – Age Ten or Under

TAMERA MOWRY

Actress & Dancer – Born July 6, 1978 – Gelhausen, West Germany
Tamera began acting at the age of 12. Since then, she has also danced in several music videos. She is the older twin by two minutes to her sister Tia. Their father was in the military, so Tamera and Tia were born in West Germany, raised in Honolulu, Hawaii, and then in 1995 moved to Los Angeles. Tamera is the bolder sibling on the hit sitcom *Sister, Sister* where she plays the part of a twin sister. She has also appeared in an episode of *Flesh N Blood, The Adventures of Hyperman, Nickelodeon's Are You Afraid of the Dark* and *Full House*. Tamera is involved with several organizations such as KidsPeace, D.A.R.E. and Make A Wish Foundation.

TIA MOWRY

Actress & Singer – born July 6, 1978 – Gelhausen, West Germany
Tia is a real-life twin who, has been performing since the age of 10. The well-rounded Tia is the singer in the family. She won the title Little Miss Texas in 1988. She enjoys inline skating, ice hockey, horseback riding, street hockey and baseball. She is currently in college studying law. As the co-star with her sister Tamera, 17 year old Tia is the obedient, neat teen in the hit sitcom *Sister, Sister*. She has also appeared in Nickelodeon's *Are You Afraid of the Dark, Full House* and *Dangerous Women*. Both Tia and Tamera have endorsed Frosted Cheerios.

TAHJ MOWRY

Actor – Born 1990 - Honolulu, Hawaii

Tahj began his career at age 4 when he appeared in a number of commercials. He made his series debut on *Who's the Boss*, and later landed a recurring role for four seasons as Teddy in *Full House*. At the age of 10, Tahj lights up the screen in his own comedy TV series *Smart Guy* on WB. He plays TJ Henderson, a naïve youngster with genius level capacities. When he was a toddler, Tahj's mom Darlene took him to watch his twin sisters Tia and Tamera at the taping of their hit sitcom *Sister, Sister*, and he got bit by the acting bug.

RIVER PHOENIX

Actor – Born August 23, 1970 – Madras, Oregon – Died October 31, 1993 – Hollywood, California

River won a series of Young Artist Awards in 1983 at age 13 for his performance in *7 Brides for 7 Brothers* which was his national film debut; in 1985 for *Surviving* and *Explorers*, in 1986 for *Stand By Me* and in 1987 for *Mosquito Coast*. He became most well-known as Chris Chambers in the classic film *Stand By Me*. He also appeared on the television show *All in the Family* and starred in the films *Hotel, It's Your Move* and, in 1993 *The Thing Called Love*.

RICKY NELSON

Actor and Singer – Born May 8, 1940 – Teaneck, New Jersey – Died December 31, 1985 – DeKalb, Texas

Ricky was the youngest son of Ozzie and Harriet Nelson. With his dad's influence as a bandleader and actor, he grew up extremely talented in music and acting. Ricky gained his fame when he was 12 years old, starring as himself on the long running family television show *The Adventures of Ozzie and Harriet*. He has also appeared in the films *Story of Three Loves* and *The Shootist* and on the television show *Streets of San Francisco*. Ricky gained major fame when he toured the world as a singer.

WILL SMITH

Rapper/Actor – Born September 25, 1968 – Philadelphia, Pennsylvania
One of the hottest performers in Hollywood today. Will Smith is also one of the most charming, In grammar school, his teachers dubbed him "Prince". Will began his career as a rap musician at the age of 12 after he met Jeff Townes (Jazzy Jeff) who dubbed him "Fresh" Prince. In 1987 Jive Records released *Rock The House*. The Fresh Prince and Jazzy Jeff later won a Grammy for *He's the DJ, I'm the Rapper*. In the meantime, Will was getting into the comedic style of Eddie Murphy and made him his role model. In 1990 Will turned toward acting with his hit TV sitcom Fresh Prince of Bel Air which ran until 1996. He then turned to a career in movies with such hit films as: *Made in America, Six Degrees of Separation, Independence Day, Men in Black* and *Enemy of the State.*

SABU

Actor – Born January 27, 1924 – Mysore, India – Died December 2, 1963
Sabu was discovered by Robert Flaherty who was shooting scenes in preparation for *The Elephant Boy*. The fearless 12 year old, Sabu was seen riding an elephant and within 24 hours, with the aid of an interpreter he was signed for the lead. Before his death, Sabu made more than 2 dozen more movies, including: *A Tiger Walks* and *Jungle Book.*

USHER

Singer and Actor – Born October 14, 1978 – Chattanooga, TN
Usher was discovered in 1992 while performing in a local talent show. At the young age of 14, he recorded his first album and became an overnight star with the release of his albums *My Way* and *Usher*. Usher has also starred in films, such as *She's All That* and *The Faculty* and appeared on the television series *Moesha.*

MALCOM JAMAL WARNER

Actor, Producer & Director – Born in Jersey City, New Jersey

Malcolm was born in New Jersey but raised in Los Angeles, where he was first introduced to acting classes. He is best known for his eight season portrayal of Theo Huxtable on *The Cosby Show*. He later went on to star in several projects including the NBC film *The Father Clements Story*, the HBO original movie *Tyson*, and the HBO movie *Tuskegee Airmen*. Malcolm's feature film debut was in the Paramount film *Drop Zone* where he played the brother of Wesley Snipe's character. Malcom began his career as a director for an episode of *The Cosby Show* and later for an episode of *Fresh Prince of Bell Air*. He has also directed several music videos and produced and directed *The Last Laugh Memories of the Cosby Show*. Among his many awards, Malcolm has received the NAACP Image Award for directing and producing the documentary *Timeout: The Truth About HIV, Aids and You* which starred Arsenio Hall and Magic Johnson. Currently, Malcolm can be seen on the hit television series *Malcolm and Eddie*.

ROBERT TOWNSEND

Actor – Born February 6, 1957

At age 16, he joined Chicago's Experimental Black Actors Guild becoming the youngest member. Through this group, he learned skills of acting and directing, and gained his first screen role in *Cooley High*. He grew up in the West side of Chicago, where he ran from a lot of gangs. So, he stayed home and watched a lot of television and was diversely stimulated by comedian Red Skelton and actor Sidney Poitier. His first film as Director was *Hollywood Shuffle* which earned more than $10 million and led him on his way. Among his many roles, he was featured in *The Mighty Quinn, The Five Heartbeats* and *Meteor Man*, to name a few. Now a filmmaker, Townsend states *"I understand the effect films and movies leave on people's lives. They affect the way we dress, comb our hair and even decorate our homes."*

VANESSA WILLIAMS

Born March 18, 1963 – Bronx, New York

Vanessa moved upstate to Millwood, NY when she was one year old. By age ten, she had immersed herself in dance and music – playing French horn, piano, and violin. Both parents were teachers and while her mother taught her about her heritage, Vanessa proudly announced that she wanted to be the first Black Rockette. Ironically, ten years later, she became the first Black Miss America. After she lost her title, she hired publicist Ramon Hervey to clean up her image and later married him. Vanessa began to record and her fist album *Right Stuff* on Polygram Records went gold. Vanessa has starred in several movies, including *Another You, New Jack City, Stompin at the Savoy,* and on Broadway in *Kiss of the Spider Woman.*

KAREN MALINA WHITE

Actress – Born in Philadelphia, PA

Known as Nicolette on the television sitcom *Malcom and Eddie,* Karen began her acting career as a student of the Philadelphia School of Creative and Performing Arts. She later graduated with a BFA from Howard University and then went to New York to pursue her acting career. Karen has had reoccurring roles on *The Cosby Show, Different World, Chicago Hope, Fresh Prince of Bel Air* and *Hanging with Mr. Cooper.* She also starred in the film *Lean on Me.* Currently, you can see Karen performing at the theatre in her one-woman show *Chain.*

JASON WEAVER

Actor – Born July 18, 1979 – Chicago, Illinois
Jason's mom Kelly Haywood is a studio singer who helped in his singing and acting career. He started acting in a Coca Cola commercial, which led to *The Jackson's: American Dream*, in which he played Michael. Following this stint. Jason landed two major roles as a singer – the voice of Simba in the *Lion King* and as Jerome Terrell in the television series *Thea*. He was also on the ABC Movie of the Week *Summertime Switch*.

SHIRLEY TEMPLE

Actress – Born 1928 – Santa Monica, California
Shirley Temple was an incredibly popular child star of the 30's who became the world's best-known child star. Known for her blond ringlets and her appealing lisp and recognized for her ability to sing and tap dance. The American public loved her with an intensity that is probably not possible to understand in the 90's. She made her debut in motion pictures at the age of 3. Her defining role was in *The Little Colonel*. By 1934 she was a full blown celebrity, starring in notable films such as: *Now and Forever, Take a Bow, Bright Eyes* and *Little Miss Marker*. At the end of that year, she was given a special Academy Award for her outstanding contribution to films. *Curly Top* and *Heidi* were other hit films. Some people believe Shirley was popular because she gave the public hope and entertainment during the depression. Shirley went on to some grownup roles, a television show and a career in politics.

RICKY SCHRODER

Actor – Born April 13, 1970 – Staten Island, New York
Ricky is one of the most successful actors ever. His first film, at the age of 9 was *The Champ*. He had been nominated several times and when he was 11 years old, he won the Young actor's Award for *Earthling* and a year later for *Silver Spoons*. Other films to his credit are: *Lonesome Dove, Out on the Edge, A Son's Promise, Crimson Tide* and *Stranger Within*. His latest role is that of Rick on *NYPD Blue*.

JOHNNY SHEFFIELD

Actor – Born April 11, 1931 – Los Angeles, California
Johnny played the boy in the *Tarzan* movies of the '40's and *Bomba* in the '50's.

BRITNEY SPEARS

Singer & Actress – Born 12/2/81 – Kentwood, Louisiana
Britney sparked her career in show business with a two year stint on the *Mickey Mouse Club* television show. Her debut album *Baby One More Time* hit #1 on the Billboard Album Charts the same week it was released. Britney has also made her acting debut with a part on *Sabrina, The Teenage Witch*.

ARTHUR REGGIE III

Actor
Arthur has spent nearly all of his young life on television. In 1994, He was Alfie Parker in the television series *My Brother and Me*. In addition he has appeared on *In Living Color* and *Sports Theater* and done voiceovers for *C. Beal and Jamal*.

BRAD RENFRO

Actor – Born July 25, 1982 – Memphis, Tennessee
Even though he had no prior acting experience or training, at age 12, Brad made an impressive debut in *The Client*. For his performance, he received the 1994 Young Actor's Award. Other films to Brad's credit include, *The Cure, Tom and Huck* (he played Huckleberry Finn) and *Telling Lies in America*. In the year 2000 his film career had escalated so much that he became in great demand, starring in several films including: *Happy Campers, Tart, Shipped Parts, Deuces Wild* and *2 Late – 2 Late*.

MARK DAKOTO ROBINSON

Actor
Mark had a role on the original *Bay Watch*. He has also starred in *Harry and the Hendersons, Back to Hannibal* and *The Return of Tom Sawyer and Huckleberry Finn*

RAFAEL ROJAS III

Actor – Born 1987
At the age of 9, Rafael played a young Greg in breaking the *Surface: The Greg Louganis Story*. He has also appeared in the films *Billboard Dad* and *7th Heaven.*

MICKEY ROONEY

Actor, Producer, Director, Writer & Singer – Born September 23, 1920 – Brooklyn, New York
Mickey had a great start in the entertainment world with both parents as actors. He made his stage debut at age 15 months as part of the family act. Mickey became well-known for a series of some 50 silent comedies which he acted in between the ages of 7 and 13, playing the character Mickey McGuire. Mickey's defining role was as the title character in the *Andy Hardy* series, including *Andy Hardy's Double Life*. Other notable films include, *Captain Courageous, National Velvet* and *Breakfast at Tiffany's*. Rooney may have made more comebacks than any other star – he has always found new audiences and new roles.

KURT RUSSELL

Actor - Born March 17, 1951 – Springfield, Massachusetts
Kurt's interest in acting came from his dad, Bing Russell, who was a baseball pro turned actor. Kurt is one of the most successful actors in show business. He started his acting career in the early 60's and managed to secure all types of roles from sweet and innocent to hardcore. Between 1964 and 1969 he appeared in *Daniel Boone* 5 times, in 5 different roles. Among his numerous film credits Kurt includes: *The Fugitive, Lost in Space, Superdad, The Quest, Escape From New York, Escape From Los Angeles, The Thing, Best of Times, Big Trouble in Little China, Tombstone*, and the list goes on.

Natori Ja'Nez   NATORI'S CLUB

Chapter 1

Is My Child Ready For TV?

Every parent has to ask themselves if their adorable little toddler or baby is really ready for the spotlight? You will know soon enough—trust me. After several auditions and feedback from producers or casting agents, you will know. The older children will tell you in some cases that they don't like it, or in some cases your child may just need a little break. Do a little homework and follow your instincts, most times they are right!! Usually the instinct that leads you to this point—to seek information on children's entertainment *is the answer*...either you knew your child was a star before their feet ever hit the ground, or someone told you that your child was a natural or talented.

Here's a checklist of some of the qualities that let you know your child is ready for television commercials?

- ❑ If your child is very outgoing and responsive when talked to?
- ❑ Does your baby smile a lot?
- ❑ Does your baby have that adorable Gerber look that could melt hearts and not just Grandma's?
- ❑ Does your child mimic or imitate what he sees on television?
- ❑ Is your baby bubbly and smiley? Does your child make silly or unusual faces?
- ❑ Is your child comfortable with strangers?

If you've answered YES to more than one of these questions, then your child is probably ready for television, commercials, print, or film.

You've just decided that you and your child are up to the challenge. OK, if you weren't scared off with all this talk of auditions, producers, and casting agents, then we're going to the next step…which is assessing your involvement in your child's new career. Remember, you're going into the entertainment business, and that's exactly what this is…a business.

5 Step Parent Checklist

The first 5 steps to the industry's door

Time

Are you willing to **take the time?** You will have to be prepared to take the time to travel to most auditions. They are not always convenient and you *must be on time*. If you are a working parent you must allow yourself time to get home, to get your child, and get back to an audition. There are some audition times that are scheduled in the evenings, so don't give up if you are a working parent, you still may be able to make some auditions. You will just have to be aware of your baby, or toddlers sleeping or eating schedule, and how it will affect them in the late afternoon or evening hours. Most younger children seem to have more energy in the morning.

Patience

Do you have the **patience?** Patience is the number one ingredient in the actor's cake. This is a "hurry up and wait" industry, from the initial stages of getting an agent to actually being on the set and filming a commercial. Make sure that you are willing to commit some time to your child's new career to go to auditions, get photos, and meet agents. This takes a lot of patience; it will all be new at first and seem like a lot of extra running around in your already *too busy* schedule. Once you get started you'll enjoy this so much—you won't even remember you were too busy.

Preparation Phase

Working documents and photos

In the beginning you will have to get a work permit and a social security card in order for your child to work. It's a very simple process and we will explain in more detail later in *Chapter III, Tools of the Trade*. In the initial stages you will begin with a small 3x5 photo that you take of your child. At a later date, if you decide to stay in the business your child will need professional photos.

Travel

Are you willing to **travel** to auditions, casting calls, and jobs? There are occasions where the auditions are 45 minutes or more away. You must be willing to arrange your schedule, after all there are no guarantees, but this could be the one.

Child's Interest

Assessing your **child's interest** in the business is a very important step. There are many children who have no interest in this business and are only doing it because you drove them there and they can't walk home. Keep in mind that your child will be away from you while auditioning and shooting commercials, make sure that your child will be able to cope with this. If not, this is

a good time to rethink this industry. The moving phrase that you will see throughout this entire book is—"is your child having fun yet?". There are various reasons that you're at this point—and they can range anywhere from you had a cute adorable tyke—to your child coming straight out of the womb with a dancing personality. You knew from birth that this was the next Smart Guy. Great, however make sure THEY also want to be "the next" just as much as you do. It is very important that you are not putting your child in the business solely for your own vicarious or selfish reasons. Why is this mentioned? Because people do it everyday, but…your child won't have any fun, and eventually you won't either. I doubt very seriously if this is you , but if by some wild chance it is…then close this book, and find another hobby or interest for your child.

Are You Ready For The Road?

Is the industry right for you?

This is a very glamorous, but extremely fickle industry. We've already asked you about your child being ready, you passed the 5 Step Parent Checklist, and again we ask: Are you ready for the road? This is the final reality check. I know of some children who have gotten into the industry and haven't missed a step. There are others who have had to wait and exercise a lot of patience in this business just to get a break. The reason is that deciding if the industry is right for you—is the most important thing you can do. For you and your child. Why? This is an industry that has been known to eat it's young. Although you can start in the business for little or nothing, you are still investing your time and some money (even if it's just gas). There's nothing worse than investing time in something and later on realizing it wasn't for you, and you could have been home knitting or doing some other really fun hobby. You as the parent must honestly assess the industry, what it has to offer, as well as your time, and your child's involvement. So, if we've haven't scared you for real this time...**You're Going into the Entertainment Business!**

The Right Look

"The Look"

The number one question asked by most parents is "Does my child have the right look?" This is a great question but it has no exact answer. The right look is whatever the client is looking for to produce their commercial, print ad, video, television show, or movie. If you look at today's shows you see a mixture of everything. This "right look" could be any child from any background, ethnicity, culture, or sex. It doesn't matter if your child is tall, thin, short, gorgeous, or the one least likely to succeed, whether you're African-American, Asian, Caucasian or Hispanic you may have the "right look" for someone's client. If you look at many commercials today and many of the programs on television, you will notice that some actors/actresses are not on there for their looks—no offense—it's just the truth. Many are there because of their talent, and the "right look" for the client. Sometimes the "right look" may be big ears, fiery red hair, special training, disability, or a special gimmick. If you remember the commercial where the lady pops her eyes out in the eye glass commercial—well she had the "right look" for that client's needs.

The Talent Club

Matching your child's talent with the industry.

Commercials and print modeling are among the easiest and most popular ways to break into the industry. However, keep your eye on your child, his or her other gifts, special talents, and what he or she has to offer. Your child may not land a commercial right away, but may be a successful print model. Your child may be very good at theatre and become a popular actor in a stage play. Some theatre acting jobs do pay for children, and that's not a terrible way to gain some additional experience, and a few extra dollars. Your son or daughter may be a great singer, and may sing their way right to the top. Let's not forget how many singers later turned to the big screen, although the vehicle was the voice. Many young talents have gotten their break on *Star Search* and other network or cable talent shows. You may have the next great dancing sensation tapping right in your kitchen. So, the bottom line is…don't limit your child. Keep all options open.

Whose Idea Is This?

Make sure you are doing this for the right reason

The $64,000 question is "Why are you doing this?" If you are doing this because you have a talented child, and your child wants this, then you are on the right track. You may then skip this entire section and fast forward to the next one. But, if you are doing this because you are planning to get rich quick, or you have any other crazy notion, or some selfish reason…finish this section and then stop right here, please close this book.

We briefly discussed this subject in assessing your **child's interest** in the business. This is very important because after talking to many agents and parents, horror stories begin when children are pushed into something they have no interest in. If you can imagine a child who dislikes a particular sport or hobby and the parent continues to push them, this usually makes the child very unhappy. When the parents find out later, they've usually spent time and money with this new hobby or interest. Everyone analyzes this fact and later says how we should have noticed, and how hindsight is 20/20. So we

just want to reiterate the fact to the parents who have particular goals in mind. Do this because you think your children will enjoy it if they are babies, do this because your children are naturals at this, do this to hone, sharpen, or expand their natural talents, do this because it may provide financial security for your child's education. That's it!! No get rich quick ideas, no pushing, no making your child do it because another one did it, or because you did it. If you push your child into this, he or she won't like it now, or later.

When you have an infant, certainly he or she won't be able to mumble the sheer disagreement of it all, but like anything else, you will see early signs of that discontentment if they really don't like it. For your older children, if they tell you they "don't want to do this, mom"…listen, it will save everyone headaches down the road. As we will repeat all throughout this book, this experience should be fun…fun…fun!

Things to Remember About Your Child's New Career

❑ Review what makes your child ready for television, film, and commercials.

❑ Review the 5 Step Parent Checklist—make sure you're ready for the industry, by investing your time and energy.

❑ Children of all types, sizes, shapes, ethnicities, and ages can work in this industry.

❑ The "right look" is the look the client is looking for.

❑ Match your child's talent with the industry.

❑ Make sure your child wants to be in this industry as much as you.

❑ Make sure your child is having fun…fun…fun!

Chapter II

Getting An Agent

Everything you always wanted to know, but don't have the time to ask!

What You Should Know About Agents

Talent Agencies are licensed by the state you are in. They register your child, accept your resumes and pictures, and they are your liaison with the entertainment world. Many talent agencies represent - clients for television, commercials, film, and modeling. They should never charge any money for the services they provide to you. Agents make their money from the client, they take their commission off the top once you are booked for the job. The usual commission is 10% percent. If anyone ever charges you money, or promises you a job once you pay—leave immediately, most likely that is a scam.

Make sure you know the difference between an agent and manager. Today's entertainment world is expanding so fast that many people are jumping on the bandwagon. There are a lot of former entertainers who think unless you are REALLY in the business making big money, you don't need a manager just yet. You will know when you need a personal manager for your child's career. My recommendation is in the initial stages you are your child's best manager. By the time you need a manager, you will know what to expect from a stranger making decisions for your child's future.

Getting An Agent

Talent Agencies

There are talent agencies in almost every city. Talent agents represent children in film, television, print and commercials. Their primary responsibility is to obtain jobs for your child. To begin, you'll need a cover letter…you will find a sample cover letter (attached). Then you will decide which agents you are going to contact first. There are listings in the Appendix of this book. That's a good place to start. There are usually agents in most cities, but if you don't have one in your city, you should be able to find one near you. If this is your very first contact with an agent, or if you are extremely new to this industry, a cover letter with a 3x5 photo of your child is sufficient. Next you'll need a copy of your child's resume. If your child has entertainment experience, or already has a resume, that's great. If they don't have one, you can construct one very easily, just review *Chapter III, Tools of the Trade*. Later in that chapter we will discuss photos in detail. If your child has already taken professional photos —feel free to enclose them along with your resume.

Many parents think that the agent makes the decision on whether your child gets into commercials, film or print ads. Quite the contrary. In fact, agents can guide you in the right direction, help you get auditions, give you advice, suggestions, and educate you on the industry, but the final decisions lay in the hands of the casting director. In some cases producers, directors and clients also decide on who makes the final cut.

Where do I find listings of Talent Agents?

This book has a thorough listing of Casting Agencies and Talent Agencies. See Appendix B on page 111. In the beginning you will concentrate on Talent Agencies, they will contact the Casting Agencies for you. The casting agency information will come in handy later down the road for other reasons. You may want to send

them some photos, or you may have an audition at a casting agency and need to find directions or know where they're located. However, in the beginning let your agent do what they do best. You can find a local list of talent agencies from the AFTRA – SAG office in your area. You can also find a list on the world wide web at http//:www.talentagency.com.

Contacting agents for the first time

For first time moms this can all seem kind of tiring. I guarantee you each step will excite you a little bit more. Here are the nuts and bolts of it…the first 5 steps.

▼ Get your child's photos

▼ Find the agencies to send them to

▼ Prepare a cover letter

▼ Prepare resume

▼ Mail self-addressed envelopes, photos, and resume, then… wait patiently.

These are five basic steps that will give you a brief overview of the best method to use when contacting agents for the first time. This is the most used method of contacting agents, however, always call the agency first and double check the procedure. Every agency has its own system and requirements. They vary a little but most of them are about the same. Each one of these steps are explained in detail in other parts of the book. We show you examples and assist you in constructing a resume and cover letter, and help you with the most efficient way to get started in show business. Most agents will ask that you enclose a self-addressed stamped envelope. Expect to receive a response from them within 4-6 weeks.

Cover letter

Your cover letter should be short and to the point. (An example is included in the Appendix A on page 104.

Most agents will ask that you enclose a self-addressed stamped envelope along with your letter and photographs. When they contact you, this is the envelope you will receive from them. You will really get excited when you recognize your own handwriting.

Next, you must decide which agents you will contact. Do a little homework first, it will save you time, heartache, and possible embarrassment later. You need to find out if they represent children, who is the person who heads up their children's department or the direct contact for children, and most important, the name of the people you should direct your mailing to. Agents sometimes move around to different agencies, and you wouldn't want to make a mistake that could have been avoided if you would have just phoned first. If you have gotten the name of an agent or agency from a friend, teacher, or a client of the agency, don't be afraid to do a little name-dropping. Be sure to include that in your cover letter. So now you've mailed off your letters and you're waiting patiently... well quite impatiently...and now you've received that letter in the mail and you're on to the next step...

Finding the right agent for you?

This is one of the necessities of show business. I have read many books that will say you must find a "good agent." That term is relative because what one person thinks is a good agent may be personal opinion. Any agent who has children in major film or television may be called a **good agent**, but is that the right agent for you? The best way is to look for the **right agent for you!**

1. Find out if they represent children.

2. Ask questions, questions, questions.

3. Find out what type of contacts and representation they have.

Your child may not be perfect for Gerber baby commercials, but may be wonderful for print ad work. Some children are great dancers or singers and may be perfect for film, modeling, or video work. Ask the agent what other types of talent they represent. Your agent should keep in contact with you. An agent should keep you updated on anything that will help you to build your child's career. Agents should work for you and your child. If for some reason they are not sending your child out, or you continue not to get jobs, then you should consider another agent. I know some parents who have exclusive contracts with an agent, and can't wait until they are over to see what else the acting world has to offer.

Babies and Toddlers

Agents who represent children also represent babies and toddlers, however, there are some agencies that specialize in representing babies. As your baby cannot talk, the most important aspect of getting representation for your little one is that charming personality, and, unfortunately, this is one time when you look for them to be friendly to strangers.

No one expects your baby or toddler to be cheery and bubbly all the time. They have their own internal clocks and nap schedules, which makes it impossible. We recommend that you do your best to schedule appointments around those times—when possible, of course. Your adorable little tykes can have "bad hair days" like everyone else.

How Do You Get Paid?

All agents get paid by commission after you get paid by the client. Their commission is approximately 10% and they take that out of the check sent to them by the clients. The agency will usually pay you within 5 working days of receiving the check.

Multi-listings and Exclusivity

Sometimes exclusivity can be a good thing—especially if your child has consistent work.

Multi-listings   Multi-listings are where you list your child with more than one agency. This is a very common practice, especially when you first get into the business. Why? This way you have the benefit of working with several different agents to see which one you really like and who fits in with you and your child. This gives your child variety and exposure to many different agents and their different clientele. Some agents get jobs that others do not, one agent may find work for you, while another one may not.

Exclusivity   Exclusivity is where you sign a contract with one agency. They are solely responsible for getting work for you, and if you solicit work on your own, they are entitled to their commission. Your agent should be giving you a substantial amount of work. If you decide to go this route, please weigh all options and make sure this is best for you and your child. In actuality, that's usually when exclusivity is considered—when there is a demand for your child. There are pro's and con's of being exclusively with one agent; this can be a great marriage if they keep you working on a regular basis. The divorce is considered when you feel your agent isn't working as hard as they can, doing their part, or you just want to change agencies. Then you must review your contract before dissolving the marriage. Please make sure you consult an attorney before, during, and after signing the contract. If you do not feel you need an attorney, make sure that you have a very good understanding of contracts.

An Interview

Rochelle McCall – McCall Model & Talent Agency

Rochelle McCall is the owner of McCall Model & Talent Agency. Rochelle comes from a strong promotional background having worked at major radio stations in the Chicagoland area and and she communted to Los Angeles quite frequently. McCall Model & Talent is a three-year-old agency that started as a home based business and has now outgrown itself into a downtown Chicago office. Rochelle represents professionals such as George Wilbourn, Jean Sparrow, Dr. Love and many other radio and television personalities, including comedians and professional athletes. She also represents Pierre Reed—a newcomer to the industry who will star in Baby Face's new movie, *Light It UP!*

As an agent, what do you feel is important for first time moms to know?

Make sure that your children want to do this. That they are not doing this because of money.

I have had parents in my office and asked their children what they like to do, and some have replied, "well I'd rather be playing baseball, but my mom's making me do this." So I just recommend that parents listen to their children.

What do you look for in children, special qualities, talents?

I like to meet children who speak for themselves, articulate well, and have a vision. It let's me know what they really want to do.

More advice to moms:

Don't burn your kids out, let them be kids. It's easy to forget that sometimes your children just want to be kids. If they want to dance, play, or be in sports, let them still have fun. Don't make them be a star, singer, or dancer unless they really want to do it. It will happen. Remember, they only have one childhood.

When at an audition or interview:

Don't speak for your child—when you start speaking that's your opinion.

Advice to children who want to get into the business:

This business is very competitive, and you must have patience. Don't put yourself down. Be able to accept the "no." If it's what you really want, eventually the doors will open. I tell people all the time, to look at Brad Pitt, he was in LA for 8 years, he was a bus boy, he waited tables and went to hundreds of auditions, and look at him now.

General do's and don'ts:

Don't get arrogant. People think that because they are in demand you have to have to get an attitude. This goes for moms of "star" children also.

How much do agents get paid for jobs?

10% for union work, and 10-15% for union jobs.

Things to Remember About Agents

❑ Make sure your agent is franchised with SAG. Never pay any money to agents, or anyone who says they will promise your child a job for money.

❑ Any unprofessional behavior can be reported to SAG.

❑ Keep your initial cover letter short and to the point.

❑ Find the right agent for your child, it will take a little bit of time, investigation, and interviewing.

❑ Agents get paid on commission for the jobs they book for you.

❑ Agents work to get you jobs, managers assist you in personal affairs, marketing, and general business matters.

❑ Always listen to your agent's advice regarding photographers.

❑ Multi-listings and exclusivity are advantageous if your agent or agents are keeping you working on a regular basis.

❑ It's OK to call them twice a week to let them know you're available.

❑ Remain patient and don't get discouraged if agents don't call as often as you would like them to.

❑ Jobs do occasionally fall through.

Chapter III

Tools of the Trade

In any business you must have tools in order to properly conduct your job. Your necessary tools are translated into working documents such as; photos and resumes. This chapter will give you step by step instructions on how to obtain your tools.

Work Documents

Work permits   Getting work permits for children varies from state to state. In some states the Department of Social Services issues them, and in other states the Board of Education issues work permits. They must be renewed twice a year. You can contact an agent in your area, through SAG, or the Department of Labor to find out where to obtain work permits in your city. The sooner you get your permit, the sooner you get started, and you are ready to get started...right? If you need any additional information regarding work permits, the agency or Social Services can usually guide you in the right direction.

Social security card   In order to work in this business, your child must have a social security number to get paid. You can get a social security card at your local social security office. If you need any additional information on how to obtain social security numbers, you can go to the local office in your area. The toll free number to the Social Security office is 800-772-1213, or they have 2 websites you can get information:

Social Security On Line
www.ssa.gov/SSA_Home.html or
Social Security Administration www.ssa.gov/

Photographs

Consider your child's photographs the entrance—your door key—to the entertainment world. In most cases your child's picture precedes your physical meeting with agents. This is one of the most important steps in your career. There are two types of photos used for this type of acting and television commercials: *Headshots and Composites.*

A *Headshot* is an 8 x 10 black and white photo. They can come in glossy and matte finishes.

A *Composite* is an 8 x 10 photo with 3 or 4 inset photos. Normally, one close up and one full length, and one other photo that shows your child's character. After you choose your photos, the most inexpensive way to reproduce them is to take them to a photo reproduction house, or reproduction service. They will print one hundred of them with your child's name and statistics on the front.

KELLYE MARSHALL

Height:	4' 7"	Dress:	7
Chest:	24	Shoe:	3
Waist:	23	Hair:	Brown
Hips:	26	Eyes:	Brown

PERSONAL PROFILE MODELING AGENCY

7530 103rd St. Suite 5
Jacksonville, FL 32210

Just remember while you're searching for a professional photographer, please find one who will take pictures that complement your child. Don't be wooed into letting Grandpop or Uncle Charlie, the resident family photographer, take pictures that will determine your child's future.

How to choose a photographer

Finding a good photographer is relatively easy because there are hundreds of them in the phone book. The best advice I have is to first ask your agent for recommendations, they see hundreds of photos daily. Another recommendation is to ask around to other moms you run into at auditions. Word of mouth is usually better than any phone book. Always look at the photographer's work, and most importantly, his work with children. If you're just starting out in the business a good photographer can be an asset.

The cost of photographs

You can spend as little as $100 or up to $500, but this is an area where you must be wise. Children's appearance changes so often that it wouldn't be wise to spend hundreds of dollars, especially when you haven't even gotten your first job. I have found that some photographers are also willing to negotiate their price, not many, but a few. Agents can also help you decide which pictures to use—they are in the business of representing your child. But, sometimes you have to use your instincts also. This is your child.

Don't make the mistake I made initially. I used my own photos for the first few years being entirely cheap and not wanting to spend the money to make my child stand out. This is a business. Headshots are nice and they also are less expensive. Composites are eye catching and separate your child—making them stand out.

The photo shoot: what to wear

The most important aspects of the photo shoot are your child's moods and personality. Schedule the appointments when your child is refreshed and rested, so your child's exuberant personality can shine. When your child goes to the photographer's studio, make sure they have at least 5 changes of clothes. Photographers always like denim, and any clothing that is comfortable. You should bring no more than one dress outfit. Denim and casual clothes work best, and remember, do not wear white or wild color prints. The photographer will shoot at least one or two rolls of film, so be prepared time wise. Most photographers will take between 24-36 pictures.

If your child has a special hobby, talent, or sports outfit bring those also. Many times props can help a lot when photographers are seeking a different or unique look. If your child is into gymnastics, basketball, martial arts, or dancing bring all outfits, uniforms, or baseballs hats add that extra look that a photographer may be looking for. After your photo shoot, your photographer will provide you with a contact sheet where you will review those pictures with your agent. If your agent is not available, or you don't have one, you may have to just use "mom instinct." Just remember that you are not choosing pictures that would just melt your heart (but usually that's all of them). You are looking for photos that show your child looking natural with a nice smile, but not too overly posed.

Photographers sometime decide to shoot outside locations, so just be prepared for everything.

First time moms only

In the very beginning it is acceptable to send a 3x5 Polaroid shot. Just a photograph of your child in comfortable clothing is fine. The child should be doing absolutely nothing other than being themselves. Agents love to see children looking natural without a lot of posing, or looking too grown-up. Please remember, don't use make-up, and don't forget to include your child's statistics on the back of the picture. Age, height, weight, color of eyes and hair.

At some point in your child's career they will have to have professional pictures done. A high-quality headshot is one of the best investments you can make in your child's career. Just remember your headshot is what will get you in doors! This is the first contact you will have with agents and casting directors. However, this is a business and your child's career. Just like any other job you want to put your best foot forward.

What type of information goes on pictures?

Name, address, date of birth, hair color, eye color. If you have room you can put the date the picture was taken, child's clothing size, and phone number.

Resumes

What information goes on your child's resume

Every child who is in the entertainment business should have a resume. They can be simple (see example). List whatever jobs, commercials, print work, plays or other work that they have. You can include anything your child has done, including pageants or plays. If your child sings, make sure you list this also. You never know when your child may be auditioning for a part that requires singing. This added talent may possibly make a difference when casting. If you have a long list of work in a particular category, list that category separately, if possible. For example: commercials, TV, film, etc. Be sure to include hobbies and church activities.

Special skills or training

If your child has any special skills, talent, or anything that makes them unique or stand out, by all means list it. If you remember the lady in the eye glass commercial obviously stood out because she could pop her eyes of the socket. Maybe not a great example, but there are many children with special talents or training who may just what the commercial or casting director is looking for.

Also remember to list any training or acting classes that they have taken.

Sample Resume

10214 S. Walden Parkway
Chicago, IL 60643

Phone 773-445-6170 or 312-617-8617
E-mail GoddessKandi@aol.com

Deminique E. Lobo

Objective

COMMERCIALS – PRINT – TV - THEATRE

Personal Information

Hair: Sandy Brown, **Eyes:** Grey, **Height:** 5,0", **Weight:** 92lbs,
Birthdate: 11-14-87   **Social Security:** 344-82-9748 **Size:** 14 **Shoe:** 6
7th grade Sutherland Elementary School

Work experience

- **Print – Print Model for Book Cover –** "Get That Cutie In Commercials:
  October 2000   Amber Books   Phoenix, AZ
- **Christmas Pajama Party at Borders Books** – Singing with her group "Kautious"
  December 1999   Borders Book Store   Chicago, IL
- **Mistress of Ceremonies** – Graduation Ceremony at Radisson Hotel, for the
  Mind Your Manners Summer Class of 99
  June 1999   Planned Events   Chicago, IL
- **The Wiz** – "Dorothy" Leading Actress & Singer
  June 1999   Sutherland Elementary School   Chicago, IL
- **MidSummer Night's Dream** – Summer Stage Production Aug. 98,
  Actress: Fairly Queen Titania
  August 1998   Theatre on the Lake   Chicago, IL
- **Cinderella** – Leading Actress
  August 1995 – 1997   Theatre on the Lake   Chicago, IL
- 95- **Tender Sweet Young Thing** – Leading Actress, Grease, & Rainbow Fish
  1994 – Present   Soloist, Model   Chicago, IL
- **Models** for Bridal shows, **Soloist** for various events Religious/Secular

Extracurricular activities

- Sutherland Basketball Team, Sutherland School Choir, Modeling, Honor Roll

Community activities

- Member of Trinity United Church of Christ
- Soloist in the Trinity United Church of Christ "Little Warriors" Choir

Awards received

- Ebony Expressions Oratorical Contest– **2nd Place** – Original Poem & Dramatic
  presentation: "Spare Change & and A Dime" – February 1999
- **Most likely to be An Opera Star** – Theatre on the Lake – August 1998
- Ebony Expressions Oratorical Contest – **1st Place** – Original Poem & Dramatic
  Presentation: "ME" – February 1997
- **Best Actress** Ilinois State Title - 1995 Miss America Pageant

Hobbies

- Acting, Basketball, Theatre, Singing, Piano, Art, Bike Riding, Track, Jumping
  Rope, Writer, Poet

Resumes should be kept short and simple, there is no need to fudge or make up jobs for your child's resume. For one thing your agent will usually find out the truth while interviewing your child, and second, it's just not worth it. Children do sometimes say the darndest things...when you least expect it!

More on resumes

When approaching agents or managers, it is always good to have a resume on file. A resume should be about one page with the basic information of last jobs, personal information such as eye color, and hair. Your agent's name should be on the resume if you have one. Agents usually have address stickers for you to use for resumes and pictures. Please list any credits, film, movies, theatre, plays, and professional training your child has.

Things to Remember About Tools of the Trade

- ❏ Work documents, photographs, resumes
- ❏ Work documents consist of a social security card and a work permit.
- ❏ Your social security number is how you get paid.
- ❏ It's imperative to get your work documents as soon as possible so that when you land a job everything will be in place. You don't want to get a job and be without work permit or social security identification.
- ❏ When looking for a photographer make sure you ask around and then look at his work.
- ❏ Make sure you use a professional photographer to get professional photos, you wouldn't want Uncle Harry, the plumber, as your professional photographer.
- ❏ A nice composite or headshot is good if you are serious about the business.

❏ Be prepared for your photo shoot with several changes of clothes.

❏ Never use make-up on your child when taking photos.

❏ Don't wear white or wild prints for photo shoots.

❏ Bring a "prop" uniform or special effect item if it is special for your child.

❏ In the beginning, it's perfectly OK to send a 3x5 snapshot.

❏ Every child in the business should have a resume.

❏ Don't fudge or fabricate information on your resume.

❏ Make sure you list any special skills, talents or training.

❏ Keep your resume short and simple.

Chapter IV

The Jobs and Opportunities

Introduction

This chapter lets you know what types of jobs and opportunities are available in the industry for babies and children. There are plenty of jobs available, but it's like any other career, you have to work at it. What is important for your child is how they look and how they act. Not how cute they are, just their specific "look". Directors, producers, clients and casting agents usually have a "look" they are searching for, and most times we don't know what that is.

The other important factor is how they respond to direction. Babies and children of all shapes sizes and ethnicities have opportunities in this business. The client just usually wants happy, healthy babies to sell their products. The baby who smiles a lot, and is comfortable or friendly in the presence of strangers will have a good career in the baby TV business. The most important thing is to keep your child working. Just remember to be patient, persistent and consistent.

For babies and toddlers only

If you watch television, then you know there are opportunities in television, commercials, and print work for babies and toddlers. Commercials are a lucrative business for babies, and they are selling everything from *Pampers* to cars. Now we know that your baby isn't driving yet, however, they can still sell cars! If you look at recent television shows and films such as *The Parent Trap 2, The Famous Jett Jackson,* and *Tarzan* you'll see that there's a place for your toddler. Commercials and print opportunities are prevalent due to hundreds of diaper commercials, baby food, diaper cremes, formula, and adult items as well. Dating back some hundreds of years we still get gooey eyed when we see babies and toddlers.

Your child will not be acting in the same manner as a ten year old, but babies and toddlers do have unique mannerisms, cute faces, character, and a good temperament. This is what sells! Most clients want healthy happy babies to sell their product. The successful baby is able to part with their parent, and is at ease around strangers. If your baby or toddler has that certain little something, that bubbly smile that everyone is always raving about, then your bubbling baby is probably right for the next diaper commercial or store advertisement. No matter what race, color, or size your adorable little one is, the jobs are available for the taking.

Twins

If you have twins you should seriously consider the business. Why? Twins or multiple children have extra benefits. If you remember back to the television show *Full House* when Mary Kate and Ashley Olsen were very young toddlers, they were switched in and out of scenes, as are most twins. Many times twins are playing the same part. This is a benefit to the producer: if one child is disagreeable or having a bad hair day...smile, he or she can be switched out of a television scene or commercial, and the show continues to go on. Some commercials call for 2 or 3 children, and when there are twins involved sometimes it's easier to cast twins and the producer gets two for one. This makes it easier for the casting director or producer. The best part, mom, is that both children get paid.

Commercials

Commercials are the easiest way for you to launch your child into the entertainment industry. How do you get your "Cutie In Commercials"? Follow the step-by-step guidelines in this book. It doesn't guarantee your child will get in the business, but it does give you heads up on the best way to approach the industry for you and your child.

Commercials are used in selling everyday products that we use on a regular basis, that's why the client is looking for "everyday kids" to sell it. This usually means children of all ethnicities and body types. An overweight child has the same chance of being in a toothpaste commercial as a thin one. Commercials can be your ticket to the film or television industry, because it's giving your child more exposure. In some cases commercials provide your child national exposure.

Photo Modeling—Print Jobs

Many of our television and commercial stars such as Brooke Shields and Halle Berry started out in modeling. Many children begin with print ads, and some children find it easier to do. It's a painless way for clients to sell everything from diapers, wet wipes, milk and toothpaste to jeans, hair ribbons and paper towels. Modeling may not be as glamorous as a commercial, but can be as lucrative. Don't be disillusioned by print work, because it's a great way to start and it leads to other opportunities. Your child's familiar face from a print ad for a major department store may lead you right into a television commercial for that same store. Many talent agents also represent models. You can send a photo with child's name, address, phone, age, weight, height, hair, and eye color, clothing size. Don't close doors, turn down money or jobs…not if they're legal.

Film

I'm sure that any child actor will jump at the opportunity to be in such great films as *Passport to Paris, Mulan, The Parent Trap 2*, and any other popular Disney films that have hit the screen. This is a once in a lifetime opportunity and if it comes your way, I say jump, but wear a life vest…translation—read the fine print, consult your agent, attorney, and business manager, but do prepare to jump. Most times you get these jobs from your agent. Every now and then you will hear a story that somebody knew somebody who knew somebody in Hollywood or they knew a casting director. The majority of the time it's a little of being in the right place at the right time, a little experience and a lot of luck! Film usually takes a little more time commitment than commercials or print ads, the bottom line here is….if **Disney calls, say yes!**

TV: Who's That Child?

There is nothing more rewarding than getting your child into a television series or sitcom. Week after week we watch such shows as *Smart Guy, Moesha*, along with many weekly cartoons that have young actors in them. This is one of the most lucrative and secure type of jobs you can get in the business. Many of the sitcoms are filmed on the west and east coasts, but you can get a break from anywhere. Watching Fox and the WB you can see that being on a regular television series can provide you with work on a long term basis. Yes, being cast in a television show is a long shot, but it's certainly worth the shot.

Voice-overs

Voice-over work for children is very popular in the film industry today. Listen closely to the voices behind many of the cartoon and Disney characters; you hear familiar voices such as: Bill Cosby on *Fat Albert*, Eddie Murphy in *Mulan*, to Roseanne, to Whoopi

Goldberg all sporting the voices to these characters. If you have listened to the voices of familiarity on such movies as *Look Who's Talking* and *Baby Geniuses*, you'll know more about voice-over work. Not to mention the addition of Disney's animated films over the past years which all must have voice-overs. Voice-overs are much like acting, but without the visual body presence. Children who do voice-overs will learn to establish a character by using their voice. Your child must be able to speak clearly, and be able to enunciate words properly, while adding drama to their voice. When your child gets an agent, it will be worth the time to get a demo tape with your child's voice and several different expressions, identities or characters.

There are agents who specialize in voice-over talent. You will also need to send your resume and demo tape to them to be considered for film, television, industrial work or cartoons. If your child has a special technique, or unique voice that stands out, this is even more of a reason to get a demo made of their voice. Have you ever heard that unique wacky voice of Bart Simpson? Would you be surprised to find out that is a woman? Your child may have a unique, squeaky, heavy or froggy sounding voice that only a mother could love—and may also be the voice of a new up and coming cartoon or Disney character. Voice-over work is quite popular and can also be lucrative, especially if your child is the voice of a long running cartoon or television sitcom. You can always submit a two-minute recording demo of your voice on tape to your agent to be considered for voice-over work. You may be pleasantly surprised.

Theatre

This is also an area where your child can gain experience and visibility. Many of the child stars have begun in musicals and major stage presentations. The opportunities are endless. The great thing about the stage is that it keeps you sharp and you can hone your skills. Plays and regular rehearsals teach discipline and responsibility. One

other thing to remember is many plays have later been turned into pilots for television, cable, or major motion picture films. The training and experience that is gained on stage can be valuable in many aspects of your child's career, they cannot be captured or bought anywhere else.

Singing and Music

Singing

If your child sings this may be a plus. The chances of your child getting a singing commercial are pretty slim, however, it may be the fact that your child sings that may be the deciding factor in a commercial that calls for singing. There are many musicals that call for children to sing. If your child is a talented singer, they may get an opportunity via an audition to sing for another type of job. I say explore all possibilities, keep all options open because you never know where they may lead. Having more than one talent is a benefit in some cases where casting directors needed a multi-talented child. There have been many roles cast for children who could act, sing, and or dance. Let's not forget that there are also many actors such as Ron Howard, and Brandy who have used their secondary talent to complement or jumpstart their other career.

Don't write your child off if they decide to pursue their singing career for a while. Just a note for your little talented songbird: many a singer or rap artist has later turned to film, television, and commercials.

Videos

The music industry is one of the most popular among children entertainers. Millions of CD's, tapes and videos are being made and listened to by children and young adults. That is why the industry is also producing more young talent such as Immature—the lead singer also being one of the stars on the hit sitcom "Sister, Sister",

N'Sync, Back Street Boys, Hanson, Blacque, and 5, just to name a few. All have early television experience. Due to the increase of these young groups, it has also increased the opportunities for music videos involving younger children who sing and dance. The twenty-first century brings younger talent and younger audiences. The music industry is very competitive, and there are thousands of great voices and musicians all over the country. Once you decide what type of music your child will specialize in, you will need the proper supporting cast. Entertainment careers and aspirations work better if it is a family decision, however that is not always possible. My best advice is for children and young adults to get as much free experience as possible, by joining church choirs, community choirs, school bands, and musicals. This helps to give your child experience, self esteem, knowledge about the industry, and what they really want to specialize in.

Music: 1-2-3's

The One-Two-Three's of the music business consist of:

▼ Getting into a studio for recording, marketing/promotion

▼ Getting your sound to the masses by way of radio stations/record stores

▼ Getting a label—not necessarily in that order

You must first get into a studio for recording. This phase is very tenuous, and there are many preparations that go into studio prep that are emotional, physical and educational. You must be prepared because studio time is very costly, it ranges from $65–$110 per hour. After your CD or tape is made, then it must be promoted and marketed. The managers work is just beginning—production, promotion, CD covers, marketing, sales, product management, finances, public relations, and legal/business affairs must all be attended to. Another recommendation is to subscribe to local and national trade publications that will keep you abreast of the

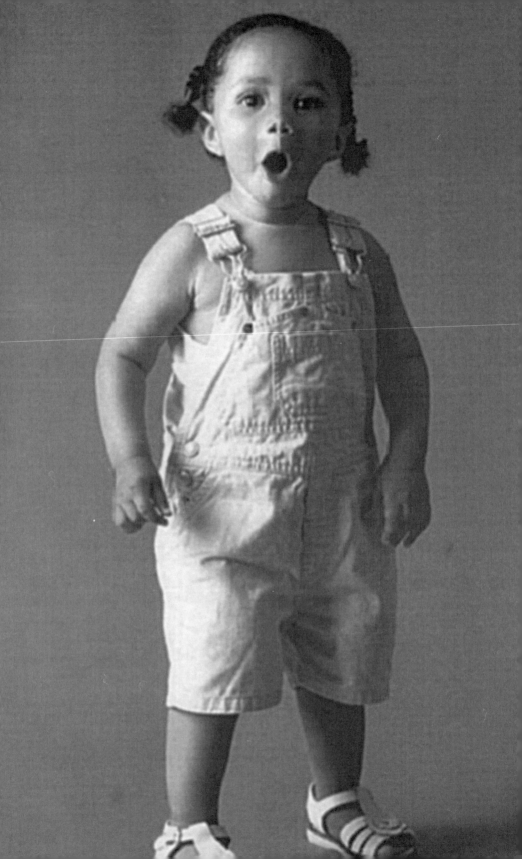

industry. I have also reminded you earlier that this is a business where everybody knows somebody, and sometimes it's their cousins uncle, brother in-law twice removed in Hollywood. Just make sure that YOU pay the most attention to all aspects of your child's career.

Your child may be just right for a musical, a commercial that calls for someone to sing, or even videos. There are infinite possibilities so make sure that when you sign up with an agency they will know all of your talents.

Hand Modeling, Body Parts

There are also other types of modeling where you use certain parts of the body only. If you have ever seen a commercial for hand lotion, and you only see a pair of hands rubbing together, this is referred to as hand modeling. These ads are also used to sell products used on knees, feet, elbows, and legs. If your child gets a job, take it, especially while in the beginning of your child's career. The more jobs on your resume the better, and you're child is gaining experience.

Dancing

There are increasing opportunities for dancers in dance videos, music videos, and musical theatre. Many theatre arts programs have dance classes included in their curriculum. Dance opportunities are not as available as acting, but they are certainly not to be discounted. Dance and music are great complimentary arts. You must also read other trade publications to keep abreast of the industry. Dance schools and universities that specialize in dance are great resources for opportunities.

Talent Comes In Many Forms
Keep Your Day Job in the Meantime!

One of the main reasons I wanted to write this book is to educate the parents, "us", that talent comes in many forms. We should not judge success on whether our child got the commercial or the part.

You should focus on the positive things you can achieve while you're awaiting your big break. First of all keep your day job, meaning keep everything in your life and your child's life the same. Keep all options open and pursue other entertainment interests. There are many other types of jobs in the entertainment world such as interactive multimedia productions, info-mercials, industrial and educational films, student and experimental films. Just make sure you keep focused, and stay grounded while you're waiting for your child's big break.

Things to Remember About Jobs and Opportunities

- ❑ Make sure you know what jobs are available in the industry.

- ❑ There are many opportunities for babies and toddlers in movies, commercials, and print ads.

- ❑ Regardless of race, color, size, looks, or ethnicity, the jobs are available.

- ❑ Twins are an asset in this business because they can double when one is not having a "bubbly day", and they are also an asset when more than one child is needed for a commercial or ad.

- ❑ Commercials are one of the easiest ways to launch your children into the entertainment industry.

- ❑ Print ads are also great ways to get your child in the business selling everything from diapers to cars. Don't close doors or turn down money.

❑ There are plenty of film and television opportunities for children today, with the influx need for family movies.

❑ Voice-over work is also very lucrative in the industry. Disney has been very instrumental in creating cartoons and animated theatre which requires the use of voiceovers. There are agents who specialize in voice-over work.

❑ Your child's singing ability is definitely a plus to their career. It may be musical theatre, or a part that calls for singing that separates them from the rest. Also remember that there are many successful singers who have turned into actors and actresses.

❑ The music industry is one of the most popular among young entertainers. Start in church or with a program that will not be expensive while you're still learning.

❑ Please consult with a professional prior to investing money in studio time and marketing.

❑ Don't rule out hand modeling and the modeling of body parts.

❑ The tap dancer, ballet or modern dancer in your house may be the next Debbie Allen, Paula Abdul, or Shirley Temple who dances or choreographs their way to the top. Read and research the dancing industry to see what opportunities are available for children.

Chapter V

Auditions, Casting, Callbacks!

Auditions: What to Expect Before, During, and After

Take pictures with you always. Once you get to the audition, sign in and then check with the casting director or their assistant. Most casting agencies will post rules, or tell you exactly what to do when you come in the office. Again, take pictures with you always, because sometimes they don't have your photo or they may want additional photographs. It also is very wise to take extra resumes. Make sure that you are always on time, yes…this can sometimes be a hurry up and wait industry, on some occasions the earlier you arrive, they earlier you may be seen, but it's always best to be on time.

Auditions

Auditions usually begin by you arranging a time with your agent to be at the casting office. When you get there, you will sign-in, get your script (if there is one), and then your child will go to the casting office. This is when you will be separated from your child, and if they think you're scared, they will be scared, so try not to show your nervousness. In most cases your agent will call you and arrange a time for you to take your child to the casting office.

Commercial Auditions

Commercial auditions are what most children start out doing. When you get to the casting agency, your child will sign in first, and then they will either be given a script, also known as "sides", or they may just videotape an impromptu screening of your child acting "au natural". Children are usually seen 5 to 10 minutes apart. Always keep your child's social security number handy. This is a very competitive market, so when your child is given a script to read, make sure they read and try to memorize the lines as well as possible. The script should be acted out; if it's a happy script or a sad script, make sure your child acts it out appropriately for the audition. Just remember to do the best you can.

Your child will be taken to the casting office where the casting director will ask some very simple questions like what school they go to, their favorite food, clothing, or a little bit about their aspirations. They should just answer these questions to the best of their ability and be themselves. When you leave make sure you sign out, and always make sure you leave some additional photos and resumes.

Remember what I said about unique or funny sounding voices. Voice-over work is popular from cartoons, to Disney to movies such as the *Tarzan* or *Toy Story*. If your child has any type of special effect or special voice technique, this would be a perfect time to show it off.

Casting and Call Backs

The casting process is broken down into several different phases. The most important thing to remember is that agents don't make decisions. Always talk to your children about being filmed, and being apart from you and make sure your child is eager, and energetic when at castings. You and your child should remain professional at all times.

Call backs

The call back happens when the casting director, producer or client likes what they saw at the audition. When you get to the "call back," you will see other people that have an interest in this project. I have seen clients, producers, and directors appear at call backs. Auditions are sometimes videotaped for later use in decision making processes. One mistake we made early on is changing outfits, always make sure your child wears the same outfit on the call back that he or she wore to the initial audition. Wear the same outfit, hairstyle, and attempt to look as much as possible like the first time, because that has a lot to do with why they called your child back.

Final calls

Producers and casting directors will probably be on hand to make decisions when you get to the final call stage. This is the audition where final decisions are made. The competition will be narrowed down to a few fierce finalists. Try to help your children to understand how important this is, but also keep them encouraged, and keep them grounded. Don't let your child be drawn into the "once in a lifetime," opportunity. They should do the best they can and have fun. Tell them there will always be a next time.

One important footnote in regard to understanding who's who in the industry, and who will make the final decision at the "final call back stage." The client hires ad agencies to advertise it's products. They contact production companies that actually make commercials, they hire casting directors who call agents...then that's where you come in. It's important to know this, because parents sometimes think that agents make decisions when most times they do not. My daughter has been on auditions where they have called in the client for final decision making.

Booking is the term used when you are hired for a job.

The Shoot and The Set

Filming a commercial can take up to an entire day. You may be surprised how much time and preparation actually goes into a 20-30 second commercial. Most commercials are shot in segments, but the producer will be there to guide them every step of the way. You and your child must be patient and remain professional at all times. Parents should never interfere, especially on the set.

SAG will give you specific information on how many hours your child can work according to the Labor Board in your state. It usually ranges between 6-10 hours per day, depending on the age of the child. Check with your local SAG office for exact hours for your child.

We've already established that your newborn has a mind and schedule of its own. So how do the producers cope with this and still make a commercial that will steal the heart of millions? There will be professionals on the set called "baby wranglers" who are specifically trained to help with young children on the set. They entertain, play, feed and nurture babies in the place of mommy. They stay with the baby to keep them happy and bubbly during and in between shoots. Most bouncy babies and toddlers will be filmed when they are having their peak personality time. The only things that will hinder a baby's performance are usually nap or feeding time. Baby Wranglers also keep the baby feeling secure since mom can't be there to cuddle them. Most babies adapt very well to their on camera experience—much better than we think.

The end rewards will be worth everything you put into it. Always be on time, try to remember to have fun. Yes…this is a hurry up and wait business sometimes…but remember you're getting paid for it.

Things to Remember About Auditions and Casting

❑ Always be on time.

❑ Once you get to the audition sign-in, check with casting for sides, or scripts or any further instructions.

❑ Make sure you take additional photos, resumes and don't forget your social security number.

❑ Commercial auditions are one of the best places for children to start in this business.

❑ When your child goes to their audition, they will separate from you, try not to show your nervousness.

❑ Commercial auditions usually last between 5-10 minutes.

❑ If you get a script, make sure your child acts it out to the best of their ability.

❑ Call backs happen when the casting director or producer likes what they see.

❑ Make sure your child wears the same outfit to the callback that he or she wore to the audition.

❑ Babies and toddlers should audition when they are having their best time of day, which is between naps and feeding schedules.

Chapter VI

Zeroing in on Your Target

This chapter will assist you in narrowing the field of your child's talents and gifts. It is very possible that your child not only came to this world with personality plus, but great looks, and is very outgoing by nature. You also knew they were stage and screen stars the moment their tiny little feet hit the floor. Your toddler or young entertainer may have several talents such as singing, dancing, and acting. The question is…which one do you pursue, choose to study or focus on. In some cases the answer is all of the above. In most cases, it may be the talent that you do not have to practice on as much, or the one that will give your child dual market ability. If your child's acting ability comes naturally, you may want to also pursue musical theatre, it may be in their best interest to study with a music or vocal coach. This chapter gives you a little additional insight on "fine tuning" those other inner talents.

Acting and Theatre Schools

This is a decision that you will have to make as a parent. Some will say that acting classes for young children are taboo, off limits, a no-no because directors don't want children who "over-act" parts at very young ages. Especially in the case of commercials; it is said that when casting directors are casting children to sell everyday products —they want everyday kids to sell it. Children who look as normal as possible.

There are two sides to this issue. Some acting instructors and program directors feel that children get life experience through arts programs. They say that there's absolutely nothing wrong with children participating in organized programs and acting classes for young children. By the age of 8 years old they will know which direction they want to take. Theatre arts programs teach them discipline, responsibility, expression, and they get to express creativity.

Musical Theatre and Vocals

There are many musicals produced by professional theatre companies, as well as many other theatrical entities. As an entertainer it is wise to "hone up" or sharpen these skills as well. This entails engaging in some sort of formal instruction. This allows you to participate in auditions feeling a strong sense of confidence. To accomplish this you may have to enroll in a school or theatre program that has dance, music, and vocal instruction. You will have the benefit of learning various art forms without the cost of individualized classes. Once you decide which one accentuates your child's talents, then you can go on to more advanced programs. Your instructor will usually have connections, recommendations, or lists of music schools that offer instructional courses for musical instrumentation. I have always been of the belief that every child should learn to play some type of musical instrument or learn to read music. You never know when your child may be at an audition and need piano skills. More importantly you want to be prepared for an acting role that also calls for a singing part. This gives your child an advantage that other kids may not have.

Voice teachers and coaches can be very helpful when trying to keep your voice trained. They really come in handy if you are auditioning for a voice part. I have also witnessed some very impressive choral ensembles for young children. They are great ways for your child to receive some professional instruction without spending an arm and a leg.

Dance Schools

Dance schools are great places for children who love dancing or want to pursue a career in dancing. There are wonderful opportunities in dance with the increasing number of dance videos that have become popular in the past years. If your child is truly interested in dancing, I would get them into a dance program, and then monitor their interest and talent closely. Many cities have major dance troupes and well known schools that have housed some of the best talent in the industry. Most teachers recommend students begin training around 8 years old. Let's not forget there are movies that also require dancing parts. Dancing is an art form that requires discipline, commitment, and patience. Mom and Dad, if your child is very agile and good at dancing, don't hesitate to get that toddler or young child in an organized program.

Books and Trade Publications

Books

If you want to get books on your craft, the best place to get them is a bookstore that specializes in books and literature for actors and theatres. You will find a few books in mainstream bookstores, but if you want the best books on the industry, look for stores that specialize in theatre books. This may also mean going to a school or university bookstore that specializes in the arts. They may have a larger variety of books specifically related to your craft. The resources it will provide will be worth the trip.

Trade Publications

The next greatest resource for actors, actresses, musicians and dancers are trade publications. These magazines will let you know what's going on in Los Angeles, New York, as well as in the entertainment business at large. They feature everything from stories, articles, and advertisements to information regarding jobs, classes, agent listings and much more. They list agencies, casting opportunities, and thorough information on availability from east coast to west coast. Although some of these publications are listed in the Appendix of this book, and you can feel free to subscribe to them, you will also find copies of them in the library or on the world wide web.

It's also a great way to find out about casting opportunities for upcoming plays. Many times they list open calls and jobs available for actors. There are also some publications that list sections just for children. Subscribe to some type of trade magazine or newsletter. Make sure some of these publications are available to you so that you can keep yourself abreast of what's happening in the industry. The bookstores also carry many new magazines that cater strictly to the arts. Just remember, this is the most updated version of life in the entertainment world, and this is **YOUR** business.

Things to Remember About Zeroing in on Your Target

❑ Narrow the field of your child's talent's by exploring, and researching which field of entertainment may be best for your child.

❑ Acting and theatre schools are not necessary for toddlers and younger children because sometimes organized classes take away their naturalness.

❑ Children who are 8 years or older may benefit from acting classes or theatre school.

❏ Musical productions are an excellent way for actresses and actors to explore double talent ability.

❏ Musical productions are especially great for actors and actresses who sing, or if your child is not quite sure which talent they want to pursue.

❏ Voice teachers and coaches are a must if you need to keep your voice trained.

❏ Dancing schools and theatre art programs are great places for children that love dance. Dancing is also a great place for children to exercise discipline, commitment, and patience.

❏ Most importantly, the best way to research and keep abreast of your industry is to read trade publications. They list the most recent jobs, schools, and information in the industry.

❏ Trade publications can be found in the back of this book, libraries, bookstores, and theatre arts stores.

Chapter VII

Joining the...Unions

What is the Union?

What is the **union**? The union is your voice to the industry. Today's union works very hard to help families adjust to the changes in the workplace and homelife. The union protects you and your rights. In the acting business, the word union is translated to AFTRA-SAG. **AFTRA** (American Federation of Television and Radio Artists), and **SAG** (Screen Actors Guild). This chapter will give you a basic overview of unions and explanations of union terminology frequently used in the business. To receive a copy of your local AFTRA-SAG booklet, check the location and call, write or check the world wide web for: AFTRA-SAG.

▼ **AFTRA** covers all aspects of free-lance theatrical/television/radio provisions for children. Everything such as: free-lance contracts on radio recorded commercials local and national, local/national national television agreements, network television agreements, public television agreements, info-mercial agreements and basic cable.

▼ **SAG** also covers free-lance contracts including: television commercials, industrial and educational contracts, public television, television motion pictures, theatrical motion pictures, interactive, info-mercial, and cable agreements.

What is Taft-Hartley?

Although Taft Hartley sounds like a distinguished partner in a major law firm, it is actually a federal statute that states: membership in a Union cannot be required by a producer as a condition of employment until 30 days after the first employment as a performer under a Union contract. After 30 days, if the performer is hired again to work again under Union contract, he/she is required in writing to join the Union, giving the non-members name, social security number and first date of employment.

AFTRA-SAG

Franchised Agents

Both AFTRA and SAG offer members lists of franchised (approved) talent agents, who may solicit employment and negotiate contracts on their behalf through such franchised talent agents. You are responsible for verifying that the agent is franchised before entering into any agency agreement. In some areas, exclusivity of representation is customary; in other areas, talent may be represented by several agents (free-lancing). An agent's commission is limited to 10% on work under the jurisdiction of Union contracts. For more information on Franchised Agents, please contact your local office.

Joining the Union

SAG ranges in the area of approximately $1,000 and AFTRA approximately $850.00 for dues. Fees are different in some regions and these amounts do not reflect the exact amount. To determine that information, please contact the AFTRA/SAG Union Membership Department. Remember, your child does not have to join until they have their first job. It is also important to remember that you must join before you work your second job, so make sure you save enough to money to join the union. You don't want to get another job and then not have enough money to join the union.

The National Offices of AFTRA/SAG are AFTRA New York: (212) 532-0800, and SAG Los Angeles: (213) 954-1600.

Labor or Pay Disputes

If you have any labor or pay disputes, you can contact the Department of Labor, the Department of Human Rights, or Better Business Bureau in your respective city or state. If you're not exactly sure who to contact, then start with the Equal Employment Opportunity Commission, National Office, 1801L Street, N.W. Washington DC, 202/663-4900, or visit their website at www.eeoc.gov.

Things to Remember About Unions

❑ The union is your voice in the industry.

❑ AFTRA-SAG is the union entity that governs the majority of entertainment industry.

❑ AFTRA is the American Federation of Television and Radio Artists.

❑ SAG is the Screen Actors Guild.

❑ AFTRA covers all aspects of free-lance theatrical /television/ radio provisions for children.

❑ SAG covers free-lance contracts including television commercials, industrial and educational contracts, public television, motion pictures info-mercial and cable agreements.

❑ Taft-Hartley is a federal statute that states: membership in a union cannot be required by a producer as a condition of employment until 30 days after the first employment as a performer under a union contract.

❑ AFTRA-SAG both offer members a list of franchised approved talent agents to solicit employment and negotiate contracts.

❑ The cost of joining the unions range in the area of $1000 for AFTRA, and $850 for SAG.

❑ For more information on joining the unions you may contact AFTRA in New York at (212) 532-0800, and SAG offices in Los Angeles at (213) 954-1600.

Chapter VIII

The Money Matters

This is one of the most important chapters in the book, especially for parents of children who begin to work on a regular basis. This chapter will answer the most frequently asked questions of parents. It will give you a brief overview of who can spend the money, how your child actor will get paid, and basic accounting information. Use it wisely and don't be too proud to hire a professional.

How Do You Get Paid?

We previously covered the commissions paid by your agent. The standard commission is 10% for agents and 15% for business managers. Agencies must pay you within 3 business days of the day they receive money from their client for theatrical work and television, 5 days for television commercials, 7 days for out-of-state checks.

Who Can Spend the Money

The money that your child earns belongs strictly to him or her. Your primary job is watch his/her money until he or she is eighteen and will then be responsible for it themselves. However, mom, you may be reimbursed a small percentage of the money for expenses. You may also be eligible for 5-15 % of money earned while your child is filming on the set. When your child starts to earn money regularly, the best advice is to hire a good accountant to assist you in keeping everything in check. You don't want to end up like those familes from the former hit television show *Different Strokes*, by not being abreast of the laws concerning spending your child's earnings.

Keeping Your Records Straight

Taxes can be very tricky, and detailed. I advise using an accountant or someone who is familiar with expenses relating to entertainment. There are write-offs and deductions that actors can take that many other professions cannot take. They can take deductions such as books, trade publications, wardrobe, drama classes, voice, music lessons, hair styling, travel expenses, and agent/manager commissions.

Do your homework, find out what is deductible. Stick to the rules, keep all of your receipts and your documentation for any monies you spend or are required to spend. Your accountant will love you for it.

Savings and Trusts

The best way to handle your child's money is to set up a trust account for your child. You can put your name or both parents' names on this trust account. It is the wisest move you can make for you and your child to ensure proper safeguarding of his/her earnings. It will separate their money from yours and it will gain interest.

FYI-The Coogan Law

There have been many parents who have misused funds earned by their child actors. Many of their stories have been seen and read in the news and in tabloids. There have been so many of these cases that the Coogan Law was instituted in 1939. The Coogan Law was named after child star Jackie Coogan, who sued his parents for misusing money he made over the years.

For those not familiar with the story, Jackie Coogan was a famous child star in the 1920's. Jackie worked with Charlie Chaplin, and worked on notable films such as *Oliver Twist* and *Robinson Crusoe*. All of this made him a millionaire before his time. As he prepared to inherit his fortune, he soon found out that his parents, who were responsible for the safe keeping of his fortune, neglected to do exactly that. Instead his mother and stepfather were living in a lap of luxury, spending his entire inheritance of over 4 million dollars. She claimed to be broke, and Coogan sued them in a Los Angeles court. In 1939, at 23 years of age, Jackie Coogan settled out of court with his mother for a mere $126,000. The Coogan Law was instituted to protect any money earned by minors in the industry working under court-approved contracts.

Things to Remember About Money

❏ Agents get 10% commission, and Managers get 15%.

❏ The money technically belongs to your child and you are just the caretakers.

❏ Hire a good accountant, especially for taxes. Actors can take deductions that others can not such as hair styling and drama classes. These deductions and write-offs can be very tricky for a novice.

❏ Keep all receipts, documents, and paperwork regarding your child's career.

❏ Savings and Trust Funds are great ways to save your child's earnings.

❏ Remember the Coogan story. Know the Coogan Law.

Chapter IX

It's About Bizness!

What is a Manager?

Managers assist you with the personal side of your child's business career. They help you with things such as public relations, and career choices. Having a manager is a big step, and one benefit is that sometimes managers are connected in the business and provide additional opportunities for you. Managers also charge about 10-15%, and fees can be negotiated for more. Make sure you know at what point to get a manager. In the beginning you can do without one until you have serious life changing decisions to make for your child. Decisions that will change your family's life such as moving out of state, signing big contracts and negotiations. When you are at the stage that you need a business manager, you will probably also need a lawyer.

When Do You Need to Hire One?

Well, to be very honest you'll know when you need to hire one. First, your child will probably making double digit thousands—$20,000 or more, and you will be increasingly having to do more "business work" for your child than your agent.

Mom, the Manager

Many parents of young entertainers are actually managing their own children. There are pros and cons to this decision. You need to be very astute in finances or legal procedures, and if you are a lawyer—that could be a plus in your camp. Let's be honest for just a minute. This is a very hard job for several reasons; first of all you and your child are now in business together. A lot of people wouldn't talk about the emotional burden that alone carries. Why? Because you're the parent, and you and the child have daily life to contend with along with the business end. It's not impossible, but be aware that's it challenging. Second, there is the issue of contracts, and financials to include money management, taxes, public relations, among other things. One very successful mom manager is Sonja Norwood, the mom of stage and song sensation Brandy. In the excerpt below, she talks of how she works hard in an industry that "eat's it young", how she keeps Brandy straight, and has been a very successful business manager.

SONJA NORWOOD is the business manager for her daughter BRANDY, singing sensation and TV star of *Moesha*.

Sonja Norwood is the business manager for one of the most popular acts in Hollywood. Her daughter, Brandy, is a singing sensation and star of *Moesha*. Quoting an excerpt from her article in *Essence* magazine article, May 1997, where Sonja says "she was determined to raise healthy, normal kids". This is an important factor in the entertainment industry. This is an industry known to put an enormous amount of pressure on anyone at it's door, and she was determined to keep her foot in there every step of the way. Her children have always been respectable, polite and well mannered. They have strong ties with the church, and she emphasizes education.

Sonja Norwood was a district manager for H & R Block, when her daughter was offered her first recording contract. Brandy has been singing since she was 2, and secured her first recording contract at 14 with Atlantic records. She decided she could do just as good a job as anyone else managing her daughter. Brandy's mother has done a wonderful job and hasn't missed a beat! Her father Willie Norwood is a talented R & B singer originally from Mississippi, and is currently the minister of music at Avalon church of Christ in Los Angeles. He is a talented musician and in charge of all musical aspects of both of his children's careers. He also accompanies them to rehearsals and recording sessions. Brandy says both of her parents constantly remind her to "keep it real." *Essence Magazine* May 1997

Here is a mom who is doing it right!!

Another successful managing mom is Pamela Warner, the mom of Malcolm Jamal Warner. So if you decide to manage your children, take some lessons from these moms.

Contracts and Contacts

In this business you will eventually have to sign a contract of some nature. It may be an exclusive contract with a talent agent, a contract for a job, or maybe a contract with a business manager. Unless you are a lawyer or a very industry savvy business person, I would enlist the services of an attorney. You don't want to sign a contract for 5 years and later find out that it will cost you more to stay in it than to get out of it, because you neglected to read the very fine print. Second, this is a business of contacts, where everybody knows somebody, and somebody knows everybody. If you have viable contacts—use them. In the meantime stick to your goals, play by the rules, and good luck!!

Things to Remember About Being a Manager

❏ Managers are personal, and they assist you with public relations, career choices, financial advice, and options.

❏ Managers charge between 10-15%.

❏ Make sure you know what point to get a manager, which is usually when you're child is making at least $20-30,000 per year, or you are doing just as much work as your child's agent.

❏ Research the responsibilities of being your child's manager before you do it.

❏ Remember it's not impossible but being your child's manager is very challenging.

❏ In order to be your child's entertainment manager, you must have full knowledge of contracts, financial entities, taxes, money management, and public relations among other things.

❑ Keep an attorney on hand to review contracts.

❑ Do your homework on other successful mothers who are managing their children, to see how they've achieved success.

Chapter X

Have A Life...

This chapter is called "Have a Life" because regardless of what happens in your child's career, YOU must maintain a "real life." This goes for you, your family, and your child actor. You must keep them in sports or whatever activities they enjoy, such as video games, sleepovers with friends, household chores, and their education. Your child must maintain social stability in church or after school programs, theatre classes—whatever will keep their life normal as possible.

Your Child's Education

Your child's education is the most important factor in this equation; education and study must be maintained at all times. While you're doing auditions everything remains fairly simple. Casting agencies sometimes have evening audition times where you can work around your child's school and your work schedule. Many times I have gone to 6:00 p.m. auditions, which has given me time to get my daughter after work, and still get to the audition. I wouldn't recommend late auditions on a regular basis, because your children are usually getting tired around that time and that may affect their performance or disposition. When auditioning, energy is very important.

Commercials fall under the same rules as auditions, in that they will not take much time out of your school schedule. Most commercials take approximately one day at most to film. You can talk with your child's teacher so that they can make up any work they missed for a one day period. Most teachers are very understanding and cooperative.

Working on the set and school

When your child is filming a television series or movie, or on the set they can get a combination of regular schooling and/or tutoring. Most will have to experience the teachers who come onto the set. Professional child actors are required to maintain at least a "C" average in order to receive a work permit. In some cases the producers are required to provide teachers to work on the set, it depends on the amount of days the child is hired to work. Some children are actually able to stay in school if the shoot is local. Teachers will determine the hours of education given to the children on the set, there is a minimum of 3 hours.

Keeping your child normal

In order to keep your child's career and mental health in tip-top shape, you should work hard to keep your child's life as normal as possible. What does that mean? If they enjoy music lessons, let them continue their lessons, time permitting. Obviously, you can't do everything, nor can you be all things to all people. You are either a very busy mom, single parent and work very hard or both. The bottom line is…the more you keep your child's life grounded, the less likely your child is to take this all so serious and personal. All the way down to the discipline factor, you must not change a thing in your child's regular schedule. Most important, don't start pampering your new star, or going overboard in awe of his or her new career. You will create a monster you won't want to deal with later. This is one of those little things that so many parents overlook until it's too late, keep abreast of that **ego**—the monster within.

It's Your Life Too...Enjoy It!!!

Your child is all over the television, or you feel like auditioning is a new part time job, and you are at home having a nervous breakdown because you weren't prepared for all this. You may have to talk to yourself occasionally (this step should not be done in the presence of others).

Along with keeping your child's life normal, it's very important that you keep your life normal as well. The two big words here are scheduling and support. There will be auditions and pop up jobs that come with the territory, but as much as possible you must do the following:

1. Keep your child on schedule.
2. Keep yourself on schedule.
3. Have a life somewhere in between.

This will be really important down the line. The worst feeling to have is to look up one day and realize that you've put so much time and energy into making this career happen for your child that it consumed you, and your family. Don't get me wrong, mom...if you're reading this, you are now saying "wait a minute...didn't you say in Chapter I that I should be committed to this project?" Yes I did, however, I am saying do not let it totally confine you or consume you. Also, mom, you must keep your health up, mentally and physically. Again, try to maintain your usual schedule. If you enjoy working out, reading, knitting, or just twiddling your thumbs twice a day, Do It!!! I also recommend daily meditation, and positive affirmations to keep YOU on track. This is a perfect time to mention support. You need a definite support system. Let's be honest—no one can do it like you can! But guess what...there's only one of you. You may have to enlist the help of a close family member, or friend to go to a few auditions, or shoots. You can't be in two places at one time. If you run into a time conflict, just enlist the help of someone who will do as good a job as you. Ask around—you'll be surprised who may come to your rescue. Parents if you're in it, be in it to win it all the way.

Ego and Attitude

It's very important to watch your child's ego and attitude. It's very possible that little Johnny or Beth could get the "big head." "Not my child." you say, and the truth is that after a big job or few commercials, it can happen most certainly. You've seen the star basketball player hit the goal winning shot, or that one great dancer that stands out at the recital. Yes, it can happen to you. Not to worry, just recognize it and put it in check while it's still early. It's the kind of small thing that can "stink" up a career real fast. If smelled by the wrong producer or casting agent, that's one piece of garlic you can do without. You don't want your child to get a negative label and have his career over before it really gets started. Just do your best to keep your child well grounded, talk to them regularly. Encourage your child every step of the way; communication is the key.

Health: Physical and Mental Well-Being

Health

For more reasons than one you should make sure you keep your child healthy. With babies and toddlers, clients like to see healthy babies to sell their products. The healthier your baby looks on that television camera or in that diaper crème commercial, the better their product will sell, and the more work your child will probably have. Babies and toddlers have unique internal scheduling that you must operate around. You must do everything you can to give your child healthy foods and plenty of exercise. Children need plenty of rest and exercise. For auditions or jobs make sure that you have healthy snacks packed in your bag, just in case you are there for longer than you expect.

Mental Well-Being

This type of career can be hard on children. Make sure you keep an eye on your child and make sure that all this action doesn't affect them negatively. If you are a loving, caring, perceptive, and intuitive parent the odds of this happening is unlikely. However, if you are pushing your child, or for some reason he doesn't really want to do this, other types of behavioral problems may manifest. Just be cautious.

Sibling Rivalry

It is very normal for siblings to become a little jealous of your budding child star. You will have to keep the peace by not showing favoritism, and making sure the lives of the other children remain just as active, normal, and stable as they always were.

I witnessed sibling rivalry between two children once where one of the children just happened to be more creatively talented than their older sibling. The mother handled it as well as anyone I've ever seen, but the oldest one acted out constantly and it was very disturbing to watch this over a number of years. There will be times that this just can't be helped, but for the most part, a nice little talk, equal discipline, no favoritism, doting or special favors to the extreme will do the trick.

Things to Remember About "Having A Life"

❑ Keep your child's life as "normal as possible"; let them continue to play ball, go to scouts, sporting events and extra-curricular activities.

❑ They must maintain their educational responsibilities regardless of jobs, auditions, or filming on a set.

❑ Teachers and tutors are available on the set when filming a job that lasts more than a couple of days.

❑ Professional children actors are required to maintain a "C" average in school

❑ Mom, you must also keep your job as normal as possible, stay healthy mentally, physically, and emotionally.

❑ Mom, keep some fun things in your life and don't get too consumed.

❑ Get a support system, you can't be two places at one time.

❑ Watch your child's ego and attitude to make sure the head doesn't get too big for the britches.

❑ Keep your child healthy, your babies and toddlers happy because clients like to see healthy, bubbly, children selling their products.

❑ Watch out for the sibling rivalry, it's normal, but don't show favoritism. Have frequent talks with all of the children, and discover the hidden talents in the others.

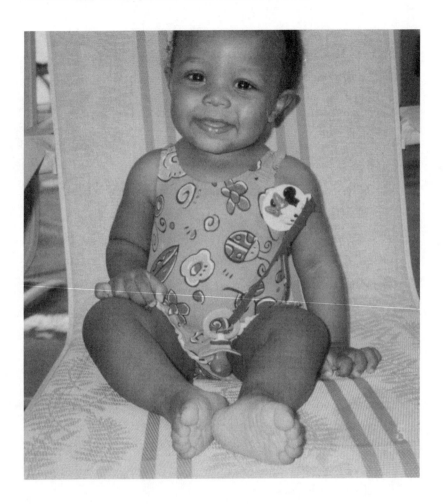

Chapter XI

For Parents Only!

This is a special chapter that candidly and openly discusses those "other" little categories that we should know about. Those terms and buzz words that we've heard people talk about, but didn't really know what they meant, or just some FYI stuff to make your child's experience a better one.

What Exactly is a Stage Mom?

Well, I've asked this question of some directors, and agents and we were told stories of moms who have similarities with fire breathing dragons. However, that part may not be quite true, but many stage moms have made a quite name for themselves. They are the ones who want the children to act. They push their children, won't let them quit when they obviously have had enough. Some say that pushy moms are the ones who get more for their kids, but there's pushing…**and there's pushing**. I think you get the point, we could go on, but we want to protect the innocent, and the not-so-guilty moms. However, if you recognize any of these traits mom, slow down, take a deep breath and let's re-group now. The good news is that it's not too late.

For first time moms it's good to read this section first so that you know now before it's too late. Make sure you learn as much as you can about the business, because that will allow you to find out the proper way to handle yourself. You will know when to coach your child, make suggestions, or just butt out. It's OK to learn from a distance. It's OK to ask questions and be concerned, but only when asked or invited to. The major players already know their parts; you may be a great writer or even a great actress in your day, but mom, this is their show—let them run it! The best thing you can do for your child is to play by the rules, their rules. It's imperative.

A Stage Dad?

Actually your job is the same as mom, just with a lot less stress. The other great thing about the stage dad is you usually don't get the stigma attached to being a "stage mom." Moms are a little more involved in this industry and the dad's role is more of encouragement and support.

Keeping It Real

What does "keeping it real" mean. This means you must be very honest with your child about the industry at all times. You must let them know how the industry works at least to the best of your ability. Tell them the truth—they won't get every job they go out for. They shouldn't think that having one commercial makes them a millionaire, and talk more in terms of saving for their education. Acting, singing, and musical talents are all their gifts. What keeps many child entertainers grounded is having "real" friends, "real" life, and all the other things in their life that they had before they were famous. By the way…one print job, or a couple of commercials doesn't usually constitute fame. It just means you've been in a commercial. We have to keep ourselves in-check in order to keep the children in-check.

Encouragement

Encouragement is one of the most important words in the emotional part of the entertainment game. The definition of encouragement is to help, relieve, comfort, embrace, inspire and support. These are

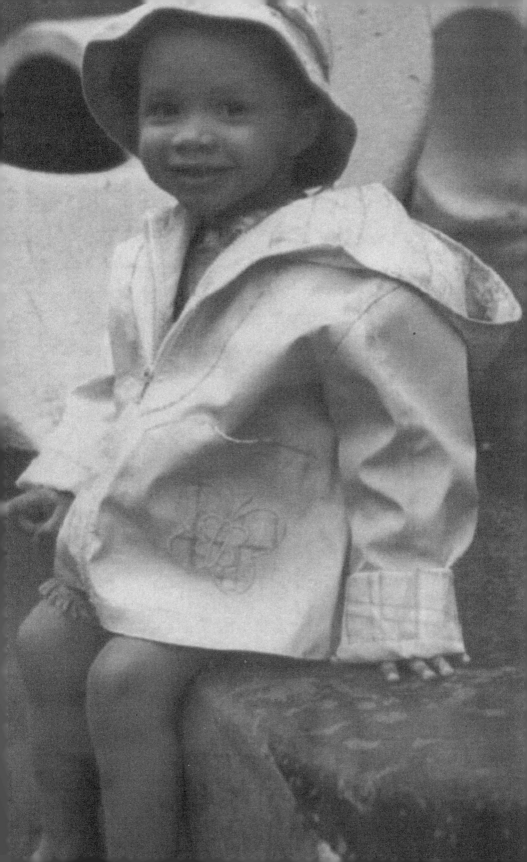

all of the words used to describe the best thing you can do for your child. Encourage and support them in this new adventure. They need all of the positive guidance you can thrust their way. In this business there will be enough days of rejection and disappointment, so mom's other job is to be an all-around, all-day support staff. It's kind of like when you start your own business, you need a few people in your corner you can lean on when the days aren't so perfect. Well mom, since you are one of the major partners in this business venture, you have to be the support staff and the cheerleading team. Be honest with your child as to what's going on, but also be encouraging without being pushy.

Some mothers can boast about being pushy as the attitude behind the altitude of their success. However, you must know the difference.

Didn't Get The Part!

Children will not get some parts, that is a certainty and it's just part of the business. It's not their fault and the feeling of rejection is part of this business. Your child will not get some parts, and sometimes they won't get the part they really want. We have to learn how to talk to them, keep encouraging them, and learn how to keep them balanced. If you tell them about the "rejection factor" up front, they won't be so devastated when they don't get that commercial they really wanted. The majority of the time when children are not chosen for a part, it's not their fault, it has more to do with the wishes of the client and the product than it does with talent. So make sure you relay this to your children early in the business, so they don't get disillusioned. I once read that this is a business for survivors. Patience and perseverance equal about 45%, timing and luck are 45%, and talent is about 10%. Now I can't say how true this is, but it sounds just like how the industry reacts. Don't get me wrong, you can't possibly prepare for everything, because your "mom power" only stretches so far…smile.

I mentioned earlier that my daughter was cast for a commercial with a well-known professional NBA basketball player in Chicago. When the shot was cancelled, she was really upset. Had we dealt with the rejection factor? Yes, had we had our talk about what happens in the business…yes. But the fact still remains that she was disappointed, this was to be her big break. It happens, and we keep on pushing to the next time.

Knowing When to Take a Break

There will come a time in your child's career when it's time to take a break, maybe even quit. Don't look at this as a negative—many times your child will want to come back, but for many reasons he or she needs to have a short rest from it all. Guess what?…Sometimes children just need to pursue other interests, or hang out with friends a little to cure this. Children must have normalcy to keep the energy going in between auditions, jobs, and life.

For new moms this doesn't apply just yet, however you will also need to know the signs…if they should appear.

Let's face it, mom, although your child may actually enjoy auditions and the jobs that comes with them, make sure you talk to your child, but listen to what your child says and observe the actions.

When is it time to take a break? The first sign is if the auditions and jobs seem like they are more work than fun. If this is becoming more of a chore for your child, you have to bribe your child to go to an audition, or they tell you they don't want to do it, listen. An old proverb said "Knowledge can be gained through the wise words of a child."

The other signs can be much more devastating; the behavioral signs. If you notice that your child is constantly not behaving while at auditions or on a job, if you notice that *his personality is not the plus* it used to be, or if his behavior is becoming unacceptable—these are signs that a problem may be on the rise. This is not to be confused with "Johnny's having a bad day." We are talking about repeated actions that tend to occur when your child is going to auditions or jobs. If your child's attitude is becoming increasingly difficult, or he or she has let you know that they don't want to do this anymore, the best thing is to let your child take a break for a while, and if nothing changes well then…that's the answer. It's probably time to let your child explore the rest of the world.

Staying Positive—The Parent

In order to succeed in this business, you, the parent, must be willing to do several things. First of all your child will go on many auditions and they may not get the commercial or ad. On the first try, the second try, or maybe even the fifth try. You have to stay positive, focused, determined and most importantly encouraging for your child.

Let's Take This Show On the Road!

Going to Hollywood or New York

Depending on how successful your child's career is going, there may come a day when you feel your child has a better chance in one of the major hubs of the entertainment world. There are many factors that would go into a move like that, namely work, not just throwing gum against the wall—but real steady work. Hopefully, what would lure you out there would be a major television contract or some other lucrative venture.

Have You Heard?

The stories about child actors who didn't make it

Child Stars   There have beenmany child stars that have had personal and professional challenges like Todd Bridges, McCaulay Culkin, and Drew Barrymore, just to name a few. Like anything else the good stories outweigh the bad; you have many child stars who have been very successful like Brandy and Malcolm Jamal Warner from the Cosby show, who now has his own sitcom and is also a television director, and producer. They have had successful careers and a successful transition to adulthood. Much of the success is credited to the parents who have done something right. They decided to have active parts in their children's career.

There are many child actors who didn't make the grade, and continue to be negative headliners such as McCaulay Culkin, Todd Bridges and a few other children, but there are many more success stories. You have Mary Kate and Ashley Olson, Brandy, Tia and Tamara Mowry and many more successful children actors. The great news is…although your child really loves this—he or she will probably not be doing this all of their lives.

Things to Remember About For Parent's Only

- ❑ "Stage Moms" can make a negative or positive name for themselves. Be known as a good "stage mom" as much as possible for your sake and your child's.

- ❑ Don't push your child too much.

- ❑ "Stage Dad" translates into stage mom without the stress.

❑ Keep it "real," be honest with your child about the industry and their expectations. Talk to them about keeping real friends, school, sports, and extracurricular activities.

❑ Encourage your child. Comfort, embrace, and support them. This will help them when the few challenging moments appear.

❑ Teach them how to handle the "rejection factor" or that feeling that comes with not getting the part.

❑ Know when to take a break, and when to quit. If your child's personality is not the plus it used to be, or your child begins to exhibit behavioral warning signs that tell you it's time for a break, then take a break. If you just listen to your children many times they will let you know.

❑ If you're ready to take that show on the road because your child is exceptionally talented, then make sure you do research and consultation. Prior to making a move like that, you must consult with your business manager, attorney, and/or agents just to cover all your bases.

Chapter XII

Exploring Other Talent Opportunities

Taking Matters In Your Own Hands

You now have an agent, your child has been going on several auditions, and you're having a little bit of disappointment because you haven't got that break yet. Give up? Absolutely not, but in the mean time and between time, you must explore other opportunities. Those opportunities may be in the form of talent showcases, churches, or other entertainment venues. Whichever, or whatever venue it may be, don't close any doors or pass up any opportunities.

Star Search

Ahhh, the illustrious *Star Searches*. Haven't all of us heard that before, and guess what else you have probably found out it's not as easy as it looks to get there. But, it is worth a try. Have I tried it? Absolutely! My daughter didn't make that cut because she was too young at the time, however, someone we know in the same group did make it all the way. It's a numbers game, and the more gum you throw against the wall, something's got to stick eventually. Again, there are many children who got the big break from *Star Searches*, so don't count it out because you never know.

Church

Some of the best talent and biggest names in the entertainment industry started out in churches. Whitney Houston, Brandy, and Mariah Carey just to name a few. The benefits far outweigh your commitment to church and your choir. If you are interested in a music career your church music director usually has resources available that can assist you in your dream. You will be surprised at the wealth of talent and resources in many churches. You may also learn some things that will help you further your gift without the burden of costs and fees.

Casting Agencies

I listed casting agencies because after you've had an agent for a while, way down the line, you may have a need to contact a casting agency. It won't hurt having the list handy for future reference, because you never know when you may need the address and information for reference material.

Talent Showcases and Cable Talent Networks

Many cities now have local talent shows and cable access talent shows. They may not all be the best quality of shows so, you want to pick the ones that you know to be up to your standard of quality, or ones sponsored by major corporations. There are many cases where local talent searches are sponsored by Oscar Meyer or other major companies who are seeking young talent. Keep your eyes and ears open for these opportunities that pop up, because usually when they do, you have to call them immediately. Keep extra pictures and resumes handy.

The Rest

Keep your eyes open for advertisements in the paper for movies being filmed in your area. Speaking of Oscar Meyer, they've been known to travel with their big hot dog through many cities looking for talent.

Local Theatre

You will find some great experience in local theatres in your area. There are great stage plays, theatres and performing arts schools in your local area that will provide opportunities you may be overlooking. There have been a few Hollywood children actors that have been discovered in their school play.

Things to Remember About Exploring Talent Opportunities

❏ If the opportunity arises, take it. More than a few not-so-talented have "struck gold", by being in the right place at the right time.

❏ Church is a usually a great way to gain experience and further your gift. Many stars have benefited from beginning in church such as; Whitney Houston, Mariah Carey, and Brandy just to name a few.

❏ You may directly contact your casting agent occasionally to let them know you're available. This is done if you've been in the business for a while and you are doing some additional marketing. This is not advised for newcomers in the business!

❏ Talent Showcases, Cable Talent shows, and Pageants are sources to pursue for broadening your talent spectrum.

❏ Oscar Meyer and other major corporations are occasionally known to hold auditions for talent, keep your eye in the papers and ears to ground.

❏ Join an entertainment company or performing arts school to keep your child's skills sharp and stay connected to the industry.

Chapter XIII

Do's & Don'ts*

Everything you should remember before going into the business.

The Parents' "21"

Final Reminders of Do's & Don'ts for a Successful Career

▼ Don't bribe or pressure your child to go to auditions. If you are at this point, it usually means you should probably take a break; it will be better in the long run for you and your child.

▼ Your photographs are your business card to the industry.

▼ Don't pay anyone who promises to "get your child into commercials."

▼ Don't use make-up on your child for pictures or photographs.

▼ Don't make your child keep going to auditions if they don't want to, or want to take a break.

▼ Please be encouraging, supportive, persistent, and optimistic all at one time. Don't be pushy.

▼ If your child wants to get out or take a break from the business—please allow him or her to do so.

▼ Don't let your child turn into a monster…if you notice they get a little big headed or start growing ears, it will show through to agents and casting directors. Be aware of egos, attitudes, and sibling rivalry.

▼ Talent comes in many forms, acting, singing, dancing, voice-overs, and photo modeling…zero in on your target.

▼ All children can work regardless of ethnicity, race, color, or size.

▼ Keep your child normal at all times, let him or her stay in sports or any other extra curricular activities.

▼ Children should maintain good health, good grades.

▼ Don't be known as **the stage mom** everyone loves to hate.

▼ Do have a three-minute monologue you keep stored in your backpack, just for that one time that an audition comes up and you'll always be prepared. It can be something you made up, most times agents have sample monologues also. You can pick up a monologue book for children from the library or most book stores. I usually just create something simple that my child is comfortable with.

▼ Children should be rested and alert when auditioning or meeting agents and managers.

▼ Read the trades regularly to keep up with the industry.

▼ Don't hesitate to send your child to acting, singing, dance, or theatre schools for additional training.

▼ Know when to join the union.

▼ Read the chapter on finances, know how to take care of the money your child will be earning.

▼ Know when to hire a manager.

▼ Mom make sure you "have a life" also, that's an order!!!

For Kids Only

If you are a child and you want to be in the entertainment field, keep these few things in mind.

▼ Just make sure that "you" want to do this.

▼ Make sure you are having fun—always.

▼ Don't be afraid to tell mom that you need a break, or maybe even you want to quit.

▼ Be yourself at interviews, auditions, and callbacks.

▼ When you don't get a part, it's not your fault.

▼ Stay encouraged and be positive, this business is hard work.

▼ Don't ever give up!!!

▼ Listen to parents, agents, directors, and producers.

▼ Stay healthy and keep up your education.

▼ Most important…Stay a kid!!!

Part 2

References

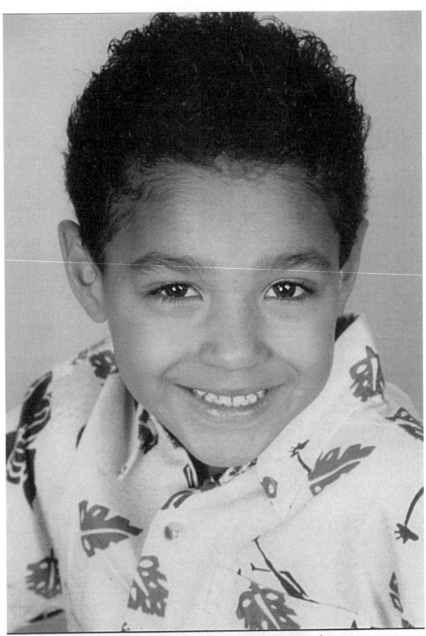

BRANDON BUTLER

Appendix A

Samples

Cover Letter

Deminique E. Lobo
10214 S. Walden Parkway
Chicago, IL 60643
(773) 445-6170/(312) 617-8617

September 3, 2000

Ms. Rochelle McCall
President
McCall Modeling & Talent Agency
233 E. Erie #208
Chicago, IL 60611

Dear Ms. McCall,

I have been recommended to your agency by Michael Humphreys, and photographer Kenneth Simmons. I am the proud mother of Deminque E. Lobo. She is a talented 11 year old actress, singer, and model. We would like to be represented by your agency.

Please find enclosed an 8x10 photograph, along with her resume'. Her composites are now being currently printed as well. I will be glad to forward additional pictures at your request. I have heard wonderful things about your agency, and I would like my daughter to be a part of it.

Demi is very outgoing, she has a great personality, she's very funny, smart, and is very eager to do commercials, television, theatre or print work. She has won pageant titles, oratorical contests, sings, and she has had leading parts in many local plays. She has also competed in some national competitions

We would like very much to meet with you in person. Thank you in advance for your time, and your consideration.

Sincerely,

Kandias Conda (mother of)
Demenique E. Lobo

Sample Contract

To Whom It May Concern:

1. I hereby employ you as my sole and exclusive representative, agent, and manager throughout the world for a term of years commencing with the date hereof.

2. Your duties hereunder shall be as follows: to use all reasonable efforts to procure employment of my services as a writer, composer, editor, author, lyricist, musician, artist, performer, designer, consultant, cameraman, technician, director, producer, supervisor, or executive and in any other capacity in the entertainment, literary, and related fields, to advise, counsel, or direct me in the development of my professional career. The aforesaid duties outside of the continental United States may, at your election, be performed by anyone else appointed by you.

3. You hereby accept this employment and agree to perform the services specified herein. You shall have the right to render your services specified herein. You shall have the right to render your services to other persons, firms, and corporations, either in a capacity in which you are hereby employed by me or otherwise. However, I agree not to employ any other person, firm, or corporation to act for me in the capacity for which I have engaged you. I hereby represent and warrant that I am free to enter into this agreement and I do not have and will not have any contract or obligation, which will conflict with it.

4. I agree to pay you as and when received by me, a sum equal to ten percent (10%) (fifteen percent (15%) with respect to any and all employment or contracts for "one-nighter" engagements or in the concert field) of the gross compensation as hereinafter defined, earned, or received by me, whether during the term hereof or thereafter, while I am

employed or compensation is received as aforesaid upon any contracts or employment, now in existence or entered into or negotiated for during the term hereof, even though payments thereon may become due or payable after the expiration of the term hereof, and upon modifications, renewals, additions, substitutions, supplements, or extensions of or to such contracts or employment, whether negotiated for during or after the term hereof. You shall be obligated to continue to serve me and perform obligations after the expiration of termination of the term hereof with respect to any employment contract and to modifications, renewals, additions, substitutions, supplements, or extensions thereof and to any employment requiring my services on which compensation is based. "Gross compensation" is defined to include all forms of compensation, money, things of value, and income (including salaries, earnings, fees, royalties, bonuses, gifts, monetary and nonmonetary consideration, securities, and shares of profits) directly or indirectly earned or received by me, or any other person, firm, or corporation in my behalf, or in which I have an interest, from my services or employment or both, and irrespective of whether the term of any such contract or employment shall be effective or continue before, during, or after the term hereof and whether or not such contract or employment was procured by you or by anyone else, and also shall include all forms of compensation, money, things of value, and income, directly or indirectly earned or received from any form of advertising or commercial tie-ups using my name, likeness, or voice. The sums due you hereunder shall be payable to you immediately upon the payment of any gross compensation to me.

5. No breach of agreement by you or failure by you to perform the terms hereof, which breach or failure to perform would otherwise be deemed a material breach of this agreement, shall be considered a material breach of this agreement, unless within ten (10) days after I acquire knowledge of such breach or failure to perform or of facts sufficient to put me upon notice of any such breach or failure to perform I serve written notice upon you of such breach or failure to perform and you do not cure said breach or failure to perform within a period of ten (10) days after receipt of said written notice by you.

6. If I fail to obtain a bona fide offer of employment from a responsible employer in the fields of endeavor above specified during a period in excess of four (4) consecutive months during the term hereof, during all of which time I am ready, able, and willing to accept employment, either party hereto shall have the right to terminate this contract by a notice in writing to such effect sent to the other party by registered mail, to the last known address of such party, provided, however, that such right shall be ineffective if after the expiration of any such four (4) month period and prior to the time I exercise such right, I have received a bona fide offer of employment from a responsible employer, and provided further that such termination shall not affect your rights or my obligations under paragraph 4 of this contract with respect to contracts or employment in existence or entered into or negotiated for prior to the effective date of such termination.

7. Insofar as this agreement refers to any employment in California, controversies arising between us under the Labor Code of the State of California, and the rules and regulations for the enforcement thereof, shall be referred to the Labor Commissioner of the State of California, as provided in Section 1700.44 of said Labor Code, save and except to the extent that the laws of the State of California now or hereafter in force may permit the reference of any such controversy to any other person or group of persons.

8. This instrument sets forth the entire agreement between us. It shall not become effective until accepted and executed by you. As an inducement to you to execute this agreement, I hereby represent and warrant that no statement, promise, representation, or inducement except as herein set forth has been made on your behalf, or by any of your employers or representatives, and I acknowledge that I have been informed that your acceptance and execution may not be changed, modified, waived, or discharged in whole or in any part except by an instrument in writing signed by you and myself. This agreement shall inure to the benefit of and be binding upon you and myself and your and my respective heirs, distributees, executors, administrators, and assigns, and you shall have the right to assign this agreement to any parent, subsidiary, affiliate, or successor entity or, pursuant to any reorganization, consolidation, combination, or merger, to any corporation, partnership, or other form. Should any provision of this agreement be void or unenforceable, such provision omitted shall remain in full force and effect.

9. Wherever the context so requires, the masculine gender shall include and apply to all genders, and the singular shall apply to and include, as well, the plural.

Very truly yours,

AGREED AND ACCEPTED:

_____(Name)

_____(Address)

TALENT AGENCY:

By_____

JADE & JAZMIN BUTLER

Appendix B

Talent Resources

African-American Talent Agencies

Most children's talent agencies will handle any child based on his or her talent and personality. The agencies listed below are exceptional in their work with African-American children.

Natori's Club
Children's Talent Agency for Print,
Catalog & Television
71 South Orange Ave, #385
South Orange, NJ 07079
Phone: 973-762-5091/973-762-5032
E-mail: acruz@natori-club.com
www.natori-club.com
Contact: Alnisia Cruz

Models Plus International
500 E. Thomas Rd., #304
Phoenix, AZ 85012
Phone: 602-234-9814
Contact: Pamela Young

Central Casting
623 Pennsylvania Ave. SE
Washington DC 20003
Phone: 202-547-6300

Atlanta Models & Talent
2970 Peachtree Road NW #600
Atlanta, GA 30305
Phone: 404-261-9627

Cameo Kids
437 Boylston St.
Boston, MA 02116
Phone: 617-536-5885

Grace Del Marco Models
350 Fifth Avenue #3110
New York, NY 10018
212-629-6404
Contact: Dee Simmons

Rage Model Management
352 Seventh Ave. #1027
New York, NY 10017
212-631-7564
Contact: Darrin Jiggetts

Visions Models
1489 Grand Concourse - #6A
Bronx, NY 10452
718-992-0301

McCall Modeling & Talent Agency
233 East Erie St. #208
Chicago, IL 60611

Sa'Rah
1935 South Halsted - #301
Chicago, IL 60608
312-751-3419

Umoja Talent Agency
2069 West Slauson Ave.
Los Angeles, CA 90047
213-290-6612

Black Model & Talent Registry
3995 East 143rd Street
Cleveland, OH 44128
216-751-7899
Contact: Bob Simpson

Bethann Management
36 North Moore Street
New York, NY 10013
212-925-2153

Ad Emphasis Model & Talent Agency
734 North LaSalle - Room 1171
Chicago, IL 60610
773-267-2530
Contact: Richard Flood

Creative Source Management
Model & Talent Agency
5510 Green Street
Philadelphia, PA 19144
215-848-1445
214-848-6611Fax
Contact: Earl D. Harvey

Talent Agencies by State

ARIZONA

Act
6264 East Grant Road
Tuscon, AZ 85712
520-885-3246

Dani's Agency
One East Camelback Road - #550
Phoenix, AZ 85012
602-263-1918

Action Talent Agency
2720 East Broadway
Tuscon, AZ 85716
520-881-6365

Leighton Agency
2231 East Camelback Road - #319
Phoenix, AZ 85016
602-224-9255

Pine Mountain Talent Agency
Prescott
520-771-1380

Fosi's Talent Agency
2777 N. Campbell Ave. - #209
Tuscon, AZ 85719
520-795-3534

Signature Models & Talent
2600 North 44th St. - #209
Phoenix, AZ 85008
602-966-1102

New Visions Modeling & Talent
Prescott
520-445-3382

Models Plus International
500 East Thomas Road - #304
Phoenix, AZ 85012
602-234-2628

Robert Black Agency
7525 E. Camelback Road - #200
Scottsdale, AZ 85251
480-966-2537

Gay Gilbert
Scottsdale
480-423-8722

Casting Unlimited
Phoenix
602-465-0315

American Celebrity Brokers
Scottsdale
602-481-2002

CALIFORNIA:
BEVERLY HILLS:

Alliance Talent, Inc
9171 Wilshire Blvd - Suite 441
Beverly Hills, CA 90210
310-858-1090

Ambrosio/Mortimer
9150 Wilshire Blvd - Suite 175
Beverly Hills, CA 90212
310-274-4274

Irvin Arthur Associates Ltd
9363 Wilshire Blvd - Suite 212
Beverly Hills, CA 90210
310-278-5934

The Blake Agency
415 N. Camden Drive, Suite 111
Beverly Hills, CA 90210
310-246-0241

Brandon's Commercials Unlimited
9601 Wilshire Blvd, Suite 620
Beverly Hills, CA 90210
310-888-8788

Capital Artists
8383 Wilshire Blvd - Suite 954
Beverly Hills, CA 90211
213-658-8118

Century Artists, Ltd
9744 Wilshire Blvd - Suite 308
Beverly Hills, CA 90212
310-395-3800

Circle Talent Associates
433 North Camden Drive - Suite 400
Beverly Hills, CA 90212
310-285-1585

Color me Bright
433 North Camden Drive - Suite 400
Beverly Hills, CA 90210
310-858-1681

Creative Artists Agency, LLC
9830 Wilshire Blvd
Beverly Hills, CA 90212
310-288-4545

Elite Model Management
345 North Maple drive - Suite 397
Beverly Hills, CA 90210
310-274-9395

Endeavor Talent Agency
350 South Beverly Blvd - Suite 300
Beverly Hills, CA 90212
310-226-8500

Epstein-Wyckoff & Associates
280 South Beverly Drive - Suite 400
Beverly Hills, CA 90212
310-278-7222

Judith Fontaine Agency, Inc
205 South Beverly Drive - Suite 212
Beverly Hills, CA 90212
310-275-4620

GVA Talent Agency, Inc.
9025 Wilshire Blvd - Suite 201
Beverly Hills, CA 90210
310-285-9552

The Gersh Agency
232 North canon Drive
Beverly Hills, CA 90210
310-274-6611

Michelle Gordon & Associates
8899 Beverly Boulevard - Suite 705
Los Angeles, CA 90048
310-288-2100

Hamilburg Agency, Mitchell J.
292 South LaCienega - Suite 312
Beveerly Hills, CA 90211

Henderson-Hogan Agency
247 South Beveerly Drive - Suite 102
Beverly Hills, CA 90212
310-274-7815/274-0751

House of Representatives Talent Agency
400 South Beverly Drive - Suite 101
Beverly Hills, CA 90212
310-772-0772

Martin Hurwitz Associates
427 North canon Drive - Suite 215
Beverly Hills, CA 90210
310-274-0240

International Creative Management
8942 Wilshire Boulevard
Beverly Hills, CA 90211
310-550-4000

The Kaplan-Stahler Agency
8383 Wilshire Boulevard - Suite 923
Beverly Hills, CA 90211
213-653-4483

Karg/Weissenbach & Associates
329 North Wetherly Drive - suite 101
Beverly Hils, CA 90210
310-205-0435

Eric Klass Agency
144 South Beverly Drive - Suite 405
Beverly Hills, CA 90212

Paul Kohner, Inc
9300 Wilshire Boulevard - Suite 555
Beverly Hills, CA 90212
310-550-1060

LW1, Inc
8383 Wilshire Boulevard - Suite 649
Beverly Hills, CA 90211
213-653-5700

The Levin Agency
8484 Wilshire Boulevard - Suite 745
Beverly Hills, CA 90211
213-653-7073

Mademoiselle Talent Agency
8693 Wilshire Boulevard - Suite 200
Beverly Hills, CA 90211
310-289-8005

Major Clients Agency
345 Maple Drive - Suite 395
Beverly Hills, CA 90210
310-205-5000

Media Artists Group
8383 Wilshire Boulevard - Suite 954
Beverly Hills, CA 90211
213-658-5050

William Morris Agency
151 El Camino Drive
Beverly Hills, CA 90212
310-274-7451

Dorothy Day Otis & Associates
373 South Robertson Boulevard
Beverly Hills, CA 90211
310-652-8855

Progressive Artists
400 South beverly drive - Suite 216
Beverly Hills, CA 90212
310-553-8561

Gilla Roos West Ltd
9744 Wilshire Boulevard - Suite 203
Beverly Hills, CA 90212
310-274-9356

Sirens Model management
9455 Santa Monica Boulevard
Beverly hills, CA 90210
310-246-1969

Susan Smith & Associates
121 North San Vincente Boulevard
Beveerly Hills, CA 90211
213-852-4777

Special Artists Agency
345 North Maple Drive - Suite 302
Beverly Hills, CA 90210
310-859-9688

Star Athlete Talent Agency
468 North Camden Drive - 2nd Floor
Beverly Hills, CA 90210
310-285-1752

Tannen & Associates
8370 Wilshire Boulevard - Suite 209
Beverly Hills, CA 90211
213-782-0515

United Talent Agency, Inc.
9560 Wilshire Boulevard - 5th Floor
Beverly Hills, CA 90212
310-273-6700

Zealous Artists P., Inc.
139 South Beverly Drive - Suite 222
Beverly Hills, CA 90212
310-281-3533

Joanne Zaluski Casting
310-456-5160

BURBANK
Burbank Media Center
818-845-3531

Casting Works, LA
818-556-6218

William Carroll Agency
139 North San Fernando Road - Suite A
Burbank, CA 91502
818-848-9948

Cavaleri & Associates
405 South Riverside Drive, Suite 200
Burbank, CA 91506
818-955-9300

Central Casting
818-569-5200

Cinema Talent Agency
2609 Wyoming ave
Burbank, CA 91505
818-845-3816

Colleen Cler Modeling
120 South Victory Blvd - Suite 206
Burbank, CA 91502
818-841-7943 / 841-4541

Disney Studios
818-560-1000

Marion Dougherty Casting
818-954-3021

Eddie Foy Casting
818-841-3003

Ellechante Talent Agency
274 Spazier Ave.
Burbank, CA 91502
818-557-3025

Gold/Marshak/Liedtke & Associates
3500 West Olive Ave - Suite 1400
Burbank, CA 91505
818-972-4300

KNBC - Channel 4
818-840-4444

Kathy & Company Casting
818-563-4121

Sarnoff Company, Inc.
3900 West Alameda Ave.
Burbank, CA 91505
818-972-1779

Jeff Meschel Casting
818-840-4729

Steven O'Neil Casting
818-840-3835

Lori Openden Casting
818-840-3774

Selected Artists Agency
3900 West Almeida Ave. - Suite 1700
Burbank, CA 91505
818-972-1747

Treadwell & Associates Casting
818-846-1666

Wallis Agency
1126 Hollywood Way - Suite 203-A
Burbank, CA 91505
818-963-4848

The Voicecaster
818-841-5300

Warner Brothers Studios
818-954-6000

CULVER CITY
Culver City Studios
310-202-1234

GMT Studios
310-649-3733

Long/Di Matteo Casting
310-841-4457

SONY Pictures Entertainment
310-280-8000

SONY Pictures Studios
310-280-6926

HOLLYWOOD
Borenstein Oreck Bogart
8271 Melrose Ave. - Suite 110
West Hollywood, CA 90046
213-658-7500

Clavie Model And Talent
7507 Sunset Blvd - Suite 201
West Hollywood, CA 90046

Coast to Coast Talent Group, Inc.
4942 Vineland Ave - Suite 200
North Hollywood, CA 91601
818-762-6278

ABC Watermark Studios
213-883-8220

Eileen Farrell/Cathy Coulter Talent
7313 Kraft Ave
North Hollywood, CA 91605
818-765-0400

The Geddes Agency
1201 Green Acre Ave
West Hollywood, CA 90046
213-878-1155

International Children's Agency
4605 Lankershim Blvd - Suite 201
North Hollywood, CA 91602
818-755-6600

Kelman/Arletta
7813 Sunset Boulevard
West Hollywood, CA 90046
213-851-8822

CFI Stage
213-460-7330

Fox Television
213-856-7000

Hollywood center Studios
213-469-5000

Charina lee Talent Agency
838 North Fairfax Ave., Suite C
West Hollywood, CA 90046
213-957-2304

Lynne & Reilly Agency
10725 Vanowen St. - Suite 113
Toluca Plaza Building
North Hollywood, CA 91605
213-850-1984

MGA/Mary Grady Agency
4444 Lankershim Blvd - Suite 207
North Hollywood, CA 91602
818-766-4414

Susan Nathe & Associates/CPC
8281 Melrose Ave - Suite 200
West Hollywood, CA 90046
213-653-7573

Cindy Osbrink Talent Agency
4605 Lankershim Blvd - Suite 401
North Hollywood, CA 91602
818-760-2488/760-0991

Clavie Model And Talent
7507 Sunset Blvd - Suite 201
West Hollywood, CA 90046

John Scagnetti Talent Agency
5118 Vineland Ave - Suite 102
North Hollywood, CA 91601
818-762-3871

Screen Artists Agency
12435 Oxnard St.
North Hollywood, CA 91606
818-755-0026

Jerome Siegel Associates
7551 Sunset Blvd - Suite 203
West Hollywood, CA 90046
213-850-1275

Richard , Sindell & Associates
8271 melrose Ave. - Suite 202
West Hollywood, CA 90046
213-653-5051

Stone Manners Agency
8091 Selma Ave
West Hollywood, CA 90046
213-654-7575

Ann Waugh Talent Agency
4731 Laurel Canyon Blvd - Suite 5
North Hollywood, CA 91607
818-890-0141

Ruth Webb Enterprises
7500 Devista Drive
West Hollywood, CA 90046
213-874-1700

K-Cal Tv Channel 9
213-467-9999

KCBS - Channel 2
212-460-3000

KCOP, Channel 13
213-851-1000

Paramount Pictures Corporation
213-956-5000

Sunset-Gower Studios, Ltd
213-467-1001

World Television
213-469-5638

Creative Image Management
213-935-7655

R. Smith Celebrity Look-Alikes
213-467-3030

Star Group Services
213-874-1239

A Prime Casting
213-962-0377

Elaine Craig Voice casting
213-469-8773

Creative Image Management
213-935-7655

LOS ANGELES
ASA
4430 Fountain Ave - Suite A
Los Angeles, CA 90029
213-662-9787

Above The line Agency
9200 Sunset Boulevard - Suite 401
Los Angeles, CA 90069
310-859-6115 / 869-6119

Abrams Artists & Associates
9200 Sunset Boulevard - Suite 625
Los Angeles, CA 90069
310-859-0625

Abrams-Rubaloff & Lawrence
8075 West Third Street - Suite 303
Los Angeles, CA 90048
213-935-1700

Acme Talent & Literary Talent
Agency
6310 San Vincente Boulevard - Suite
520
Los Angeles, CA 90048
213-954-2263

Agency For Performing Arts
9000 Sunset Boulevard - Suite 1200
Los Angeles, CA 90069
310-273-0744

The Agency
1800 Avenue of the Stars - Suite 400
Los Angeles, CA 90067
310-551-3000

ABC Television Center Studios
213-557-7777

Carthay Center Studios
213-908-2101
A.C. Casting
213-782-9314

Anderson/McCook/White Casting
310-659-5535

Allen Talent Agency
11755 Wilshire Blvd - Suite 1750
Los Angeles, CA 90025
213-896-9372

Carlos Alvarado Agency
8455 Beverly Blvd - Suite 441
Beverly Hills, CA 90048

Amsel Eisenstadt & Frazier
6310 San Vincente Blvd - Suite 401
Los Angeles, CA 90048
213-939-1188

Angel City Talent
1680 Vine St - Suite 716
Los Angeles, CA 90028
213-463-1680

Artist Network
8438 Melrose Place
Los Angeles, CA 90069
213-651-4244

Artists Agency
10000 Santa Monica Blvd. - Suite 305
Los Angeles, CA 90067
310-277-7779

Artists Group Ltd
303 South Crescent Heights
Los Angeles, CA 90048
213-656-1025

Badgley & Connor
9229 Sunset Boulevard - Suite 311
Los Angeles, CA 90069
310-278-9313

Baier-Kleinman International
3575 West Cahuenga Blvd - suite 500
Los Angeles, CA 90068
818-761-1001

Bauman, Hiller & Associates
5757 Wilshire Blvd - Penthouse 5
Los Angeles, CA 90036
213-857-6666

Sara Bennett Agency
6404 Hollywood Blvd - Suite 327
Los Angeles, CA 90028
213-956-9666

Lois Benson
8360 Melrose Ave - Suite 203
Los Angeles, CA 90069
213-653-0500

BCI Casting
213-951-1010

Brown/West Casting
213-938-2575

J. Michael Bloom & Associates
9255 Sunset Boulevard - 7th Floor
Los Angeles, CA 90069
310-275-6800

Nicole Bordeaux Talent Agency
616 N. Robertson Blvd - 2nd Floor
Los Angeles, CA 90069
310-289-2550

Paul Brandon & Associates
1033 North Carol Drive - Suite T-6
Los Angeles, CA 90069
310-273-6173

Don Buchwald & Associates
9229 Sunset Blvd
Los Angeles, CA 90069
310-278-3600

Iris Burton Agency
1450 Belfast Drive
Los Angeles, CA 90069
310-652-0954

CL Inc
843 North Sycamore Ave
Los Angeles, CA 90038
213-461-3971

CNA & Associates
1925 Century Park East - Suite 750
Los Angeles, CA 90067
310-556-4343

Caro Jones Casting
213-664-0460

Casting Company
213-938-0700

Casting Society of America
213-463-1925

CHN International Agency
213-874-8252

The Chasin Agency
8899 Beverly Boulevard - Suite 716
Los Angeles, CA 90048
310-278-7505

Chateau Billings Talent Agency
5657 Wilshire Boulevard - Suite 340
Los Angeles, CA 90036
213-965-5432

Jack Chutuk & Associates
10586 Chevlot Drive - Suite 700
Los Angeles, CA 90067
310-552-1773

Colours Model & Talent Management
8344 1/2 West Third St.
Los Angeles, CA 90048
213-658-7072

Christal Blue Casting
213-654-7717

The Cosden Agency
3518 West Cahuenga Blvd - Suite 216
Los Angeles, CA 90068
213-874-7200

The Craig Agency
8485 Melrose Place - Suite E
Los Angeles, CA 90069
213-655-0236

Susan Crow & Associates
1010 hammond St - Suite 102
Los Angeles, CA 90069
310-859-9784

Cunningham, Escott & Dipene
10635 Santa Monica Blvd - Suite 102
Los Angeles, CA 90025
310-475-2111

DH Talent Agency
1800 North Highland Ave - Suite 300
Los Angeles, CA 90028
213-962-6643

DZA Talent Agency
8981 Sunset Blvd - Suite 503
Los Angeles, CA 90069
310-274-8025

The Devroe Agency
6311 Romaine Street
Los Angeles, CA 90038
213-962-3040

Dytman & Schwartz Talent Agency
8200 Sunset Boulevard - Suite 809
Los Angeles, CA 90069
310-274-8844

Divisek Casting
213-876-1554

Favored Artist Agency
122 South Robertson Blvd - Suite 202
Los Angeles, CA 90048
310-247-1040

Ferrar-Maziroff Associates
8430 Santa Monica Blvd - Suite 220
Los Angeles, CA 90069
213-654-2601

Film Casting Associates
310-657-8457
Flashcast Kids
818-760-7986

Flick East & West Talents, Inc
9057 Nemo St, Suite A
Los Angeles, CA 90069
310-271-9111

Barry Freed Company
2029 Century Park East - Suite 600
Los Angeles, CA 90067
310-277-1260

Alice Fries Agency
1927 Vista Del Mar Ave
Los Angeles, CA 90068
213-464-1404

Future Agency
8929 S. Sepulveda Blvd - Suite 314
Los Angeles, CA 90045
310-338-9602

GRA/Gordon Rael Agency, LLC.
9255 Sunset Blvd - Suite 404
Los Angeles, CA 90069
310-285-9552

The Gage Group, Inc.
9255 Sunset Blvd - Suite 515
Los Angeles, CA 90069
310-859-8777

Helen Garrett Talent Agency
6435 Sunset Blvd
Los Angeles, CA 90028
213-871-8707

Dale Garrick International
8831 Sunset Blvd - Suite 402
Los Angeles, CA 90069
310-657-2661

Jan Glaser
310-820-6733
Goldman & Associates
213-463-1600

Joe Guinan & Associates
213-782-6968

Hispanic Talent Casting
213-934-6465

Don Gerler Agency
3349 Cahuenega Blvd - Suite 1
Los Angeles, CA 90068
213-850-7386

Goldey Company Inc
116 North Robertson Blvd - Suite 700
Los Angeles, CA 90048
310-657-3277

Greene & Associates
8899 Beverly Blvd - Suite 705
Los Angeles, CA 90048
310-288-2100

HWA Talent Representatives
1964 Westwood Blvd - Suite 400
Los Angeles, CA 90025
310-446-1313

Haeggstrom Office, Talent Agency
6404 Wilshire Blvd - Suite 1100
Los Angeles, CA 90048
213-658-9111

Buzz Halliday & Associates
8899 Beverly Blvd, Suite 620
Los Angeles, CA 90048
310-275-6028

Halpern & Associates
12304 Santa Monica Blvd - Suite 104
Los Angeles, CA 90025
310-571-4488

Vaughn D. Hart & Associates
8899 Beverly Blvd - Suite 815
Los Angeles, CA 90048
310-273-7887

IFA Talent Agency
2049 Century Park East - Suite 2500
Los Angeles, CA 90067
310-659-5522

Innovative Artists
1999 Ave of the Stars - Suite 2850
Los Angeles, CA 90067
310-553-5200

IT Model Management
528 North Larchmont Blvd
Los Angeles, CA 90004
213-962-9564

Jeow Entertainment, Talent Agency
1717 North Highland Ave - Suite 805
Los Angeles, CA 90028
213-468-9470

JS Represents, Talent Agency
509 North fairfax Ave. - Suite 216
Los Angeles, CA 90036
213-653-2577

George Jay Agency
6269 Selma Ave - Suite 15
Los Angeles, CA 90028
213-466-6665

Alan Kaminsky
213-463-1600

Kerwin William Agency
1605 North Cahuenga Blvd - Suite 202
Los Angeles, CA 90028
213-469-5155

Victor Kruglov & Associates
7060 Hollywood Blvd - Suite 1220
Los Angeles, CA 90028
213-957-9000

LA Talent
8335 Sunset Blvd - 2nd Floor
Los Angeles, CA 90069
213-656-3722

Lenhoff/Robinson Talent Agency
1728 South LaCienega Blvd.
Los Angeles, CA 90035
310-558-4700

Levy, Robin & Associates
9220 Sunset Blvd - Suite 303
Los Angeles, CA 90069
310-278-08748

Liberman/Hirschfield
213-525-1381

Robert Light Agency
6404 Wilshire Blvd - Suite 900
Los Angeles, CA 90048
213-651-1777

Ken Lindner & Associates
2049 century Park east, Suite 2750
Los Angeles, CA 90067

Los Angeles Premiere Artists Agency
8899 Beverly Blvd - Suite 510
Los Angeles, CA 90048
310-271-1414

Lovell & Associates
7095 Hollywood Blvd - Suite 1006
Los Angeles, CA 90028
213-876-1560

Jana Luker Talent Agency
1923 1/2 Westwood Blvd - Suite 3
Los Angeles, CA 90025

Lund Agency
3330 Barham Blvd - Suite 103
Los Angeles, CA 90068
818-508-1688

Malary International
10642 Santa Monica Blvd - Suite 103
Los Angeles, CA 90025
310-234-9114

Manning Casting
213-852-1046

Malaky International
10642 Santa Monica Blvd. - Suite 103
Los Angeles, CA 90025
310-234-9114

Metropolitan Talent Agency
4526 Wilshire Boulevard
Los Angeles, CA 90010
213-857-4500

Miramar Talent Agency
7400 Beverly Blvd - Suite 220
Los Angeles, CA 90036
213-934-0700

H. David Moss & Assoc.
735 North Seward St - Penthouse
Los Angeles, CA 90038
213-465-1234

Next Management Company Talent
Agency
662 North Robertson Boulevard
Los Angeles, CA 90069
310-358-0100

Pakula King & Associates
9229 Sunset Boulevard - Suite 315
Los Angeles, CA 90069
310-281-4868

Paradigm Talent Agency
10100 Santa Monica Blvd. - Suite 2500
Los Angeles, CA 90067
310-277-4400

The Partos Company
6363 Wilshire Boulevard - Suite 227
Los Angeles, CA 90048
213-876-5500

Perseus Modeling & Talent
3807 Wilshire Boulevard - Suite 1102
Los Angeles, CA 90010
213-383-2322

Players Talent Agency
8770 Shoreham Drive - suite 2
Los Angeles, CA 90069
310-289-8777

Privilege Talent Agency
8170 Beverly Boulevard - Suite 204
Los Angeles, CA 90048
213-658-8781

Pro-Aport & Entertainment Company
11661 San Vincente Blvd - Suite 304
Los Angeles, CA 90049
310-207-0228

Quality Artists
5455 Wilshire Boulevard - Suite 1807
Los Angeles, CA 90036
213-936-8400

Renaissance Talent & Literary Agency
8523 Sunset Boulevard
Los Angeles, CA 90069
310-289-3636

Stephanie Rogers & Associates
3575 West Cahuenga Blvd - Suite 249
Los Angeles, CA 90068
213-851-5155

New Age Casting
213-782-9313

Paradoxe Casting
213-655-3492

Principal Casting
213-782-3966

The Marion Rosenberg Office
8428 melrose Place - Suite B
Los Angeles, CA 90069
213-653-7383

Barbara Rensen & Associates
213-464-7968

Lila Selik Casting
310-556-2444

SDB Partners, Inc
1801 Avenue of the Stars - Suite 902
Los Angeles, CA 90062
310-785-0060

The Sanders Agency
8831 Sunset Boulevard - Suite 304
Los Angeles, CA 90069
310-652-1119

The Savage Agency
6212 Banner Ave
Burbank, CA 91505
818-972-1779

Stuart Stone Casting
310-820-9200

Schiowitz/Clay/Rose, Inc.
1680 North Vine Street - Suite 614
Los Angeles, CA 90028
213-463-7300

Sandie Schnarr Talent
8500 Melrose Ave. - Suite 212
Los Angeles, CA 90069
213-653-9479

Judy Schoen & Associates
606 North Larchmont Blvd - Suite 309
Los Angeles, CA 90004
213-962-1950

Don Schwartz Associates
6922 Hollywood Blvd. - Suite 508
Los Angeles, CA 90028
213-464-4366

Shapiro-Lichtman, Inc.
8827 Beverly Boulevard
Los Angeles, CA 90048
310-859-8877

The Shumaker Talent Agency
6533 Hollywood Boulevard - Suite 401
Los Angeles, CA 90028
213-464-0745

Silver, Massetti & Szatmary/West Ltd.
8730 Sunset Blvd - Suite 440
Los Angeles, CA 90069
310-289-0909

Stuart Stone Casting
310-820-9200

Michael Slessinger Associates
8730 Sunset Boulevard - Suite 220
Los Angeles, CA 90069
310-657-7113

Starwill Talent Agency
6253 Hollywood Blvd - Suite 730
Los Angeles, CA 90028
213-874-1239

Teschner Casting
310-557-5542

Charles H. Stern Agency
11766 Wilshire Boulevard - Suite 760
Los Angeles, CA 90025
310-479-1788

Peter Strain & Associates
8428 Melrose Place - Suite D
Los Angeles, CA 90069
213-782-8910

Sun Agency
8961 Sunset Boulevard - Suite V
Los Angeles, CA 90069
310-888-8737

Sunset West Models, Talent Agency
8490 Sunset Boulevard - Suite 502
Los Angeles, CA 90069
310 -659-5340

Sutton, Barth & Vennari Inc.
145 South Fairfax Ave. - Suite 310
Los Angeles, CA 90036
213-936-6000

Talent Group, Inc.
6300 Wilshire Blvd - Suite 2110
Los Angeles, CA 90048
213-852-9559

Thomas Talent Agency, Inc.
6767 Forest Lawn Drive - Suite 101
Los Angeles, CA 90068
213-850-6767

Turning Point Talent Agency
6601 Center Drive West - Suite 500
Los Angeles, CA 90045
310-348-8171

Umoja Talent Agency
2069 West Slauson Ave.
.Los Angeles, CA 90047
213-290-6612

Vision Art Management
9200 Sunset Boulevard - Penthouse 1
Los Angeles, CA 90069
310-888-3288

Erika Wain Agency
1418 North Highland Ave. - Suite 102
Los Angeles, CA 90028
213-460-4224

Shirley Wilson & Associates
5410 Wilshire Boulevard - Suite 227
Los Angeles, CA 90036
213-857-6977

Carter Wright Enterprises
6513 Hollywood Boulevard - Suite 900
Los Angeles, CA 90024
310-824-6300

YBA Enterprises, Talent Agency
8380 Melrose Ave. - Suite 311
Los Angeles, CA 90069
213-655-7245

Stella Zadeh & Associates
11759 Iowa Ave.
Los Angeles, CA 90212
310-281-3533

COLORADO
Donna Baldwin Talent
50 South Steele St - #260
Denver, CO 80209
303-320-0067

Maximum Talent
3900 East Mexico Ave. - #105
Denver, CO 80210
303-691-2344

Barbizon Agency
7535 East Hampden - #108
Denver, CO 80231
303-337-6952

Jeanine's Modeling & Talent
Colorado Springs
719-598-4507

CONNECTICUT
Media Inc
West Hartford
203-523-4388

Patrick Media Productions
Hartford
203-522-8118

Johnston Agency
South Norwalk
203-838-6188

World Promotions
New Haven
203-781-3427

126

Barbizon Agency
Stamford
203-359-0427

Faces and Places
Weston
203-221-1400

DELAWARE
Robert Taylor
Wilmington
302-217-3675

The May Studio
Bear
302-845-3048

DISTRICT OF COLUMBIA
Capital Casting
202-797-8621

Central Casting
623 Pennsylvania Ave. SE
Washington, DC 20003
202-547-6300

T-H-E Artist Agency
202-342-0933

Doran Agency
202-333-6367

Stars Casting
202-429-9494

FLORIDA
A-1 Peg's Talent Agency
133 E. Lauren Court
FernPark, FL 32730
407-834-0406

Act One Talent Agency
1205 Washington Ave.
Miami Beach, FL 33139
305-672-0200

Boca Talent & Model Agency
851 North Market St
Jacksonville, FL 32202
904-356-4244

Flick East-West Talents, Inc.
919 Collins Ave.
Miami Beach, FL 33139
303-674-9900

Alexa Model & Talent
4100 West Kennedy Blvd. - #228
Tampa, FL 33609
813-289-8020

Green Agency, Inc.
1688 Meridian Ave. – 8th Floor
Miami Beach, FL 33139
407-644-0600

Dott Burns Model & Talent
478 Severn Ave – Davis Island
Tampa, FL 33606
813-251-5882

International Artists Group, Inc.
420 Lincoln Road - #382
Miami Beach, FL 33139
305-538-6100

Strictly Entertainment, Inc.
813-879-1514

Irene Marie Agency
728 Ocean Drive
Miami Beach, FL 33139
305-672-2929

Evelyn Stewart's Modeling
1765-B West Fletcher Ave.
Tampa, FL 33612
813-968-1441

305-Page Parkes Models
660 Ocean Drive
Miami Beach, FL 33139
305-672-4869

Louise's People Model & Talent Agency
863 13th Ave. North
St. Petersburg, FL 33701
813-823-7828

Michele Pommier Models, Inc.
81 Washington Ave.
Miami Beach, FL 33139
305-531-5886

Martin & Donald Talent Agency
1915 A Hollywood Blvd
Hollywood, FL 33020
954-921-2427

Sheffield Agency, Inc.
800 West Ave. - #C-1
Miami Beach, FL 33139
305-531-5886

Famous Faces Entertainment Company
954-922-0700

Stellar Talent Agency
407 Lincoln Road - #2K
Miami Beach, FL 33139
305-672-2217

Young Faces Unlimited
708 NE 7th St.
Hallandale, FL 33009
305-454-7711

Ford Models
305-534-7200

Elite Model Management – Miami
305-674-9500

Just For Kids Talent Agency
1995 NE 150th St.
North Miami, FL 33161
305-940-1311

Florida Stars Model & Talent
225 West University Ave. – Suite A
Gainesville, FL 32601

World of Kids
1460 Ocean Drive - #205
Miami Beach, FL 33183
305-672-5437

Suzanne Haley Talent
618 Wymore Road - #2
Winter Park, FL 32789

Swift Kids
1400 Ocean Drive
Miami Beach, FL 33183
305-672-9882

Dimensions 3 Modeling
5205 South Orange Ave - #209
Orlando, FL 33020
407-851-2575

Amazing Kids Inc
420 Lincoln Road
Miami Beach, FL 33139
305-532-1118

Anderson Jess Productions & Modeling
10661 North Kendall Drive
Miami, FL 33176
305-279-1190

Black Models Network
1655 Drexel Ave.
Miami, FL 33139
305-531-2700

GEORGIA

Atlanta Models & Talent
2970 Peachtree Road NW - #600
Atlanta, GA 30305
404-261-9627

Kiddin Around Models & Talent
1479 Spring St NW
Atlanta, GA 30309
404-872-8582

AW/Atlanta
887 West Marietta St -#N-101
Atlanta, GA 30318
404-876-8555

Genesis Models & Talent
1465 Northside Drive - #120
Atlanta, GA 30318
404-350-9212

Atlanta' s Young Faces
6075 Roswell Road NE
Atlanta, GA 30328
404-255-3080

The People Store
2004 Rockledge Road NE - #60
Atlanta, GA 30324
404-874-6448

Ted Borden & Associates
2434 Adina Drive NE - #B
Atlanta, GA 30324
404-266-0664

Young Expressions
Atlanta
404-691-0122

Elite Model Management
181 14th St - #325
Atlanta, GA 30309
404-872-7444

Hot Shot Kids
3300 Buckeye Road
Chamblee, GA 30341
770-986-9600

Glyn Kennedy Models & Talent
3500 Emperor Way
Atlanta, GA 30084
770-908-9082

Tara Modeling & Talent with Kidz
650 Morrow Industrial Boulevard
Jonesboro, GA 30236
770-968-7700

HAWAII

ADR Model & Talent Agency
431 Kuwill St.
Honolulu, HI 96817
808-524-4777

Amos Kotomori Agent Services
1018 Hoawa Lane
Honolulu, HI 96826
808-956-6511

Kathy Muller Talent Agency
619 Kapahula Ave – Penthouse
Honolulu, HI 96815
808-737-7917

Chameleon Talent Agency
Maui
808-879-7817

IDAHO

Gretchen Palmer
208-788-4501

Tamara Lynne Thompson
208-343-0038

Terry Ryan
208-529-0976

Sunny Anderson Casting
406-933-8461

ILLINOIS

All-City Casting
312-296-9268

Susanne's A-Plus Talent
108 West Oak St. - #406
Chicago, IL 60610
312-943-8315

Chambliss Casting
312-278-9123

McCall Modeling & Talent Agency
233 E. Erie, #208
Chicago, IL 60611

Voice's Unlimited
541 North Fairbanks Court - #28
Chicago, IL 60611
312-642-3262

Sa-rah
1935 South Halsted - #301
Chicago, IL 60608
312-733-2822

Salazar & Navas, Inc.
760 North Ogden Ave. - #2200
Chicago, IL 60622
312-751-3419

Norman Shucart Enterprises
1417 Green Bay Road
Highland Park, IL 60035
847-433-1113

Arlene Wilson Talent
430 West Erie St. - #210
Chicago, IL 60610
312-573-0200

Kidz Casting
312-943-9303

North Shore Talent
450 Peterson Road
Libertyville, IL 60048
847-816-1811

Stewart Talent Management
212 West Superior St. - #406
Chicago, IL 60610
312-943-3131

Elite Model Management
312-943-3226

INDIANA

C. J. Mercury, Inc.
1330 Lake Ave.
Whiting, IN 46394
219-659-2701

Artists Enterprises
Indianapolis
317-577-1717

Helen Wells Agency
Carmel
317-843-5363

Act 1 Agency
Indianapolis
317-255-3100

Charmaine Model Agency
Fort Wayne
317-485-8421

Taylor Nichols, Inc.
Indianapolis
317-255-2996

IOWA
Greg Schmidt
Cedar lake
515-357-5177

Winning Combinations
Des Moines
515-287-2100

International Group
Cedar Rapids
319-369-0639

Dennis Hitchcock
Rock Island
309-786-4119

Complete Casting
Des Moines
515-276-0170

Performance Film, Video & Stage
West Des Moines
515-221-2514

KANSAS
Jackson Artists
7251 Lowell Drive - #200
Overland Park, KS 66204
913-384-6688

Lorraine Young-Yocum
Independence
816-833-2272

Talent Unlimited
4049 Pennsylvania - #300
Kansas City, KS 64111
816-561-9040

All Star Casting
Lake Lolawana
913-831-9953

Agency Models & Talent
Kansas City
913-342-8382

Jackson Artists Corp
Overland Park
913-384-6688

Wright/Laird Casting
Kansas City
816-531-0331

KENTUCKY
Eben Henson
Danville
606-236-2747

Images
Lexington
606-273-2301

Tillie Moore
Lexington
606-266-0789

Stage One Children's Theatre
Louisville
502-589-5946

Vogue of Lexington
Lexington
606-254-4582

Youth Performing Arts High
Louisville
502-454-8355

LOUISIANA
Stephanie Brett Samuel
New Orleans
504-895-5666

New Orleans Model & Talent
New Orleans
504-525-0100

Rick Landry Casting
New Orleans
504-454-8000

Model & Talent Management
Baton Rouge
504-295-3999

Faces Model & Talent Mgmt
New Orleans
504-522-3030

Victor's International Talent
Metairie
504-885-3841

Fame Model & Talent Agency
New Orleans
504-522-2001

MARYLAND
Fox Enterprises
7700 Little River Pike - #200
Amandale, MD 22003
703-506-0335

Central Casting
Baltimore
410-889-3200

Kids International Talent Agency
938 East Swan Creek Rd - #152
Fort Washington, MD 20744
301-292-6093

Camera Ready Kids
Silver Springs
301-589-4864

Taylor Royall Agency
2308 South Road
Baltimore, MD 21209
410-466-5959

Young Professionals
Silver Spring
301-567-0831

Call All Kids
Baltimore
301-970-2170

MASSACHUSETTS
Rose Agency
Bedford
617-275-9084

Outcasting
Brookline
617-738-6322

Boston Casting
Boston
617-864-9749

Nadette Stasa Casting
Cambridge
617-864-1344

Boston Model Club Kids
Boston
617-247-9020

Boston Agency for Children
380 Broadway
Somerville, MA 02111

Cameo Kids
437 Boylston St.
Boston, MA 02116
617-536-5885

MICHIGAN
Affiliated Models
1680 Crooks Road - #200
Troy, MI 48084
810-244-8770

Mary Locker Casting
Detroit
313-366-4942

Productions Plus
30600 Telegraph Road - #2156
Birmingham, MI 48025
810-644-5566

Elizabeth Grayson Models
Garden City
313-421-9009

The Talent Shop
30100 Telegraph Road - #116
Birmingham, MI 48025
810-644-4877

Action Casting
Huntington Woods
810-398-3027

Hollywood Stars Management
Detroit
313-818-4357

Pro Talent Agency
Grand Rapids
616-458-2513

MINNESOTA
Midwest Connections
Duluth
218-727-0997

Eleanor Moore Agency
Minneapolis
612-827-3823

Creative Casting Talent
Minneapolis
612-375-0525

Portfolio Models & Talents
Minneapolis
612-338-5800

Kimberly Franson Talent
Minneapolis
612-338-1605

Meredith Model & Talent Agency
St. Paul
612-298-9555

MISSISSIPPI
Connections Casting
Jackson
601-354-3542

Debbie Edge
Tupelo
601-365-8873

Jack Stevens
Jackson
601-355-7535

Delta Talent
Clarksdale
601-624-6956

MISSOURI

Lorraine Young Yocum
Independence
816-833-2272

Wendy Gray
Kansas City
816-931-5828

Talent Unlimited
St. Louis
816-561-9040

Wright-Laird Casting
Kansas City
816-531-0331

Carrie Houk
St. Louis
314-862-1236

Talent Plus, Inc.
55 Maryland Plaza
St. Louis, MO 63108
314-367-5588

MONTANA

Creative World
Billings
406-259-9540

Montana Mystique Talent Agency
Bozeman
406-586-6099

NEBRASKA

Talent Pool Inc
Omaha
402-455-3000

Helen Blume
Omaha
402-556-1359

NEVADA

J. Baskow & Associates
2948 East Russell Road
Las Vegas, NV 89120
702-733-7818

Premiere Models
Las Vegas
702-733-6888

Creative Talent Agency
900 East Karen Ave - #D-116
Las Vegas, NV 89109
702-737-0611

Donna Wauhob Agency
3135 Industrial Road - #234
Las Vegas, NV 89109
702-733-1017

Lenz Agency
1591 East Desert Inn Road
Las Vegas, NV 89109
702-733-6888

Lear Casting
Las Vegas
702-459-2090

NEW HAMPSHIRE
Concord Community Music School
Concord
603-228-1196

New Hampshire Theatre Project
Portsmouth
603-431-6644

NEW JERSEY
Veronica Goodman Agency
411 Route 70 East - #240
Cherry Hills, NJ 89034
609-795-3133

Adine Duron
Upper Montclair
201-744-5698

McCullough Associates
8 South Hanover Ave.
Margate, NJ 89402
609-822-2222

Shirley Grant Mangement
Teaneck
201-692-1653

Weist/Barron/Ryan
Atlantic City
609-347-0074

Robert Taylor Talent
Lindenwold
609-346-1763

Swann & Associates
Newark
201-621-7331

Talent Marketing
Clifton
201-779-0700

Natori's Club
Childrens Talent Agency
71 South Orange Ave. - #385
South Orange, NJ 07079
973-762-5032
Attn: Alvisia Cruz

Special Artists Management
Red Bank
908-758-9393

NEW MEXICO
Aesthetics Inc
489 ½ Don Miguel
Sante Fe, NM 87501
505-982-5883

The Mannequin Agency
2021 San Mateo Blvd. NE
Albuquerque, NM 87110
505-266-6823

Applause Talent Agency
225 San Pedro NE
Albuquerque, NM 87108
505-262-9733

The Phoenix Agency
6400 Uptown Blvd NE - #481 W
Albuquerque, NM 87110
505-881-1209

Cimarron Talent Agency
10605 Casador Del Oso NE
Albuquerque NM 87111
505-292-2314

South of Sante Fe Talent Guild
6921-B Montgomery NE
Albuquerqe, NM 87109
505-880-8550

Eaton Agency
2626 High St NE
Albuquerque, NM 87107
505-344-3149

Casting House
Sante Fe
506-988-3624

NEW YORK
A Plus Agency
18 West 21st St., 7th Fl.
New York, NY 10010

Abrams Artists & Associates
420 Madison Ave – 14th Floor
New York, NY 10017
212-935-8980

Carson/Adler Agency, Inc.
250 West 57th St - #729
New York, NY 10107
212-307-1882 / 212-541-7008

Agency for Performing Arts
888 Seventh Ave. – 6th Floor
New York, NY 10106
212-582-1500

Epstein-Wyckoff & Associates
311 West 43rd St. – 304
New York, NY 10036
212-586-9110 / 212-586-8019

Associated Booking Corporation
1995 Broadway
New York, NY 10023
212-874-2400

Frontier Booking International, Inc.
1560 broadway – Suite 1110
New York, NY 10036
212-221-0220

Richard Astor Agency
250 West 57th St. - #2014
New York, NY 10107
212-581-1970

Ford Children
344 East 59th St
New York, NY 10022
212-688-7613

Amerifilm Casting
212-334-3382
Maureen Fremont Casting
212-302-1215

Carol Baker Agency
165 West 46th Street – Suite 1106
New York, NY 10036
212-719-4013

Cunningham, Escott & Dipene
257 Park Ave. South, 9th Fl.
New York, NY 10010
Attn: Halle Feldstein
212-477-1666

Ford Children's Division
142 Greene St.
New York, NY 10012
Attn: Wendy/Andrea

Funnyface Today
151 E. 31st St., #24J
New York, NY 10016
Attn: Babies/Children

The Gage Group
315 West 57th St. - #411
New York, NY 10019
212-541-5250

J. Michael Bloom & Associates
233 Park Ave South – 10th Floor
New York, NY 10003
212-529-6600 / 212-529-5838

Gilchrist Talent Group
630 Ninth Ave - #800
New York, NY 10036
212-692-9166 / 212-953-4188

Baby Wranglers Casting Company
212-736-0060

Judy Henderson & Associates
212-877-0225

Jerry Beaver & Associates
212-979-0909

Hispanicast
212-691-7366

Jane Brinkler Casting
212-924-3322

Hyde-Hamlet Casting
718-783-9634

Henderson/Hogan Agency
850 Seventh Ave - #1003
New York, NY 10019
212-765-5190 / 212-586-2855

Generation Model Management
20 West 20th St.
New York, NY 10011
212-721-7219

Ginger Dicce Talent Agency
1650 Broadway, #714
New York, NY 10019

Jan J. Agency Inc
365 West 34th St – 3rd Floor
New York, NY 10001
212-967-5265

Dorothy Palmer Talent Agency
235 West 56th St - #903
New York, NY 10001
212-766-4280

Jordan Gill & Dorinbaum Talent Agency
156 Fifth Ave. – Suite 711
New York, NY 10010
212-463-8455 / 212-691-6111

McDonald Richards, Inc.
156 Fifth Ave. #222
New York, NY 10010

Product Model Management
240 West 35th St
New York, NY 10001
212-563-6444 / 212-465- 1967 fax

Judy Keller Casting
212-463-7676

Michael Amato Agency
212-247-4456

Joan Lynn Casting
212-675-5595

Rachel's Talent Agency
134 West 29th St - #903
New York, NY 10001
212-967-0665

Fifi Oscard Agency, Inc.
24 West 40th St - #17
New York, NY 10018
212-764-1100 / 212-840-5019

Gilla Roos Ltd
16 West 22nd St – 7r¹
New York, NY 1ͨ
212-727-78ͨ

)01

Vision Models
1489 Grand Concourse - #6A
Bronx, NY 10452
718-992-0301

Schiffman, Ekman, Morrison and Mark
22 West 19th St – 8th Floor
New York, NY 10011
212-627-5500

Rage Model Management
352 7th Ave - #1027
New York, NY 10001
212-631-7564

Schuller Talent/N.Y. Kids
276 Fifth Avenue #1001
New York, NY 10001
Attn: Margaret Martuka

Ellen Novack Casting
212-431-3939

Rechael's Totz & Teens
134 West 29th St
New York, NY 10001
212-967-3167

Kids Power Model & Talent
161 West 16th St.
New York, NY 10011

Talent Representatives, Inc
20 West 53rd St
New York, NY 10022
212-752-1835

Adele's Kids & Adults
212-608-4300

Chicky's Kids
212-288-0140

Mc Donald/Richards
156 Fifth Ave - #222
New York, NY 10011
212-627-3100

Madison Talent Group
310 Madison Ave - #1508
New York, NY 10017
212-922-9600

Zoli Management
3 West 18th St – 5th Floor
New York, NY 10011
212-242-7480

William Morris Agency
1325 Avenue of the Americas
New York, NY 10014
212-586-5100

Navarro/Bertoni & Associates
212-736-9272

Pyramid Entertainment Group
89 Fifth Ave
New York, NY 10003
212-242-7274

Swift Kids
49 West 37th St
New York, NY 10018
2-997-1785

New York Kids
276 Fifth Ave – 10th Floor
New York, NY 10001
212-532-6005

Petite Kingdom Agency
San Juan
787-723-3270

SOUTH CAROLINA
Ernest Mitchell
Columbia
803-252-6575

Brenda Cook
Charleston
803-722-6720

George Corell
Greenville
864-299-1101

Margaret Mullins
Charleston
803-853-8738

Marcia Weissman
Hilton Head
803-681-8023

Sheila Dixon
Columbia
803-782-7338

SOUTH DAKOTA
Black Hills Talent & Booking
Rapid City
605-341-5940

Bernice Johnson Modeling
Sioux Falls
605-388-3918

Inter-Mountain Entertainment
Rapid City
605-348-7777

Professional Image by Rosemary
Sioux Falls
605-334-0619

TENNESSEE
Actors and Others Talent Agency
6676 Memphis-Arlington Road
Bartlett, TN 38134
901-385-7885

Talent & Model Land
4516 Granny White Pike
Nashville, TN 37204
615-321-5596

Box Office, Inc Talent Agency
1010 16th Ave. South
Nashville, TN 37212
615-256-5400

Talent Trek Agency
406 11th St.
Knoxville, TN 37916
423-977-8735

Creative Artists Agency
3310 West End Ave. – 5th Floor
Nashville, TN 37203
615-383-8787

Creative Communities
Memphis
901-458-3900

Buddy Lee Attractions
38 Music Square East - #300
Nashville, TN 37203
615-244-4336

People of Color Talent Agency
Memphis
901-372-3733

The Talent Connection
Nashville, TN
615-831-0039

Robbins Model & Talent
Memphis
901-761-0211

William Morris Agency
2100 West End Ave - #1000
Nashville, TN 37203
615-385-0310

Colors Talent Agency
Memphis
901-523-9900

TEXAS

Acclaim Partners
4107 Medical Parkway - #207
Austin, TX 78756
512-323-5566

Actors, Etc.
2620 Fountainview - #210
Houston, TX 77057
512-785-4495

Third Coast Casting
Austin
512-472-4247

Lucille Graham Casting
Houston
713-522-6703

Shirley Abrams
Dallas
214-484-6774

Intermedia Talent Agency
5353 West Alabama - #222
Houston, TX 77056
713-622-8282

Dallas Casting Company
Dallas
214-416-4455

Pastorini BosbyTalent Agency
3013 Fountain View Drive - #240
Houston, TX 77057
713-266-4488

Mary Collins Agency
Dallas
214-360-0900

Quaid Talent Agency
5959 Richmond - #310
Houston, TX 77057
713-975-9600

Marge Moody Casting
San Antonio
210-492-9688

Sherry Young Agency
2620 Fountain View - #212
Houston, TX 77057
713-266-5800

Sinclair Talent International
San Antonio
210-614-2281

Rona Lamont Casting
Houston
713-785-0465

UTAH
Act-1
Salt Lake City
801-277-9127

The Casting Company
Salt Lake City
801-467-7544

Hailie Talent Agency
Salt Lake City
801-532-6961

Models International
Salt Lake City
801-942-8485

Elite Media Talent Management
Salt Lake City
801-539-1740

Walker Talent Agency
Salt Lake City
801-363-6411

VIRGINIA
Capital Casting
Arlington
202-797-8621

Applause Unlimited
Richmond
804-264-0299

Fox Enterprises
Falls Church
703-506-0335

Sherri L. Goodwin
Richmond
804-321-2684

Wright Agency
Newport News
804-886-5884

KLP Casting
Richmond
800-480-8031

Chris Taylor Casting
Norfolk
804-625-2278

The Model Shoppe
Richmond
804-278-8743

Talent Connection
Norfolk
804-624-1975

Modelogic
Richmond
804-644-1000

Richmond Modeling Registry
Richmond
804-359-1331

Uptown Talent, Inc.
Richmond
804-740-0307

WASHINGTON
Actors Group
114 Alaskan Way South - #104
Seattle, WA 98104
206-624-9465

Carol James Agency
117 South Main St
Seattle, WA 98104
206-447-9191

E. Thomas Bliss & Associates
219 1st Ave South - #420
Seattle, WA 98104
206-340-1875

ABC Kids –N-Teens
114 Alaskan Way South
Seattle, WA 98104
206-646-5440

Dramatic Artists Agency
1000 Lenora St - #501
Seattle, WA 98121
206-442-9190

Kids Team
911 East Pike St - #210
Seattle, WA 98122
206-860-8688

Lola Hallowell Agency
1700 West Lake Ave North - #600
Seattle, WA 98109
206-281-4646

Kids Biz Talent Agency
Bellevue
206-455-8800

Young Performers Studio
Seattle
206-989-9080

ABC Kids-N-Teens
1028 Gravely Lake Drive SW
Tacoma, WA 98499
206-581-2680

WEST VIRGINIA

Kanawha Players
Charleston
304-925-5051

Lakeview Theater
Morgantown
304-598-0144

McHugh Management
Charleston
304-776-6768

Image Associates
South Charleston
304-345-4429

David Wohl Casting
Charleston
304-766-3186

Kellas-Grindley Productions
Wheeling
304-242-5201

WISCONSIN

Cameron Casting
Madison
608-251-3907

Jennifer's Talent Unlimited
Milwaukee
414-277-9440

Gered International
Madison
608-238-6372

Kandi International
Milwaukee
414-264-8931

Images International Model Mgmt
Milwaukee
414-476-5980

Arlene Wilson Management
Milwaukee
414-778-3838

WYOMING
Hamilton Casting
Cheyenne
307-637-5771

Lisa Samford Casting
Wilson
307-733-3613

Hughes Production Company
Jackson
307-733-6505

Wyoming Talent & Modeling Agency
Casper
307-266-6427

Real People Casting
Moose
307-733-8857

New York Casting Directors

The following casting director's are in New York & vicinity. Please don't phone or visit if indicated by *. **Note:** photos & resumes will not be returned.

AMERIFILM CASTING *
375 Broadway #3R
New York, NY 10012
212-334-3382

BASS-VISGILLiO CASTING *
648 Broadway #912
New York, NY 10012
212-598-9032

BREANNA BENJAMIN CASTING *
13 East 37th Street
New York, NY 10018
212-213-4753

JAY BINDER CASTING *
321 West 44th Street - #606
New York, NY 10036

JANE BRINKER CASTING LTD *
51 West 16th Street
New York, NY 10011

KRISTINE BULAKOWSKI
CASTING *
Prince Street Station
P.O. Box 616
New York, NY 10012
212-769-8850

CTP CASTING *
22 West 27th Street - 10th Floor
New York, NY 10001

DONALD CASE CASTING INC. *
386 Park Avenue South #809
New York, NY 10016
212-889-6555

COMPLETE CASTING *
350 West 50th Street
New York, NY 10019
212-265-7460

BYRON CRYSTAL
41 Union Square West #316
New York, NY 10003

SUE CRYSTAL CASTING *
251 West 87th Street - Suite 316
New York, NY 10003

DONNA DE SETA CASTING *
525 Broadway - 3rd Floor
New York, NY 10012

SYLVIA FAY *
71 Park Avenue
New York, NY 10016

LEONARD FINGER *
1501 Broadway
New York, NY 10036

DENISE FITZGERALD CASTING
111 East 12th Street - Suite A-1
New York, NY 10003
212-473-2744

JUDIE FIXLER CASTING
P.O. Box 149
Green Farms, CT 06436-0149
203-254-4416

GODLOVE & SINDLINGER
CASTING *
151 West 25th Street - 11th Floor
New York, NY 10001
212-627-7300

AMY GOSSELS CASTING *
1382 Third Avenue
New York, NY 10021
212-472-6961

MARIA & TONY GRECO
CASTING *
630 North Avenue #702
New York, NY 10036

JOEY GUASTELLA CASTING *
85-10 151st Avenue #5B
Queens, NY 11414
718-835-6451

CAROL HANZEL CASTING *
39 West 19th Street
12th Floor
New York, NY 10011
212-242-6113

HEDGES-HOFFMAN CASTING *
525 South 4th Street #246
Philadelphia, PA 19147
215-829-9001
215-829-0505 Actor Hotline

JUDY HENDERSON CASTING
330 West 89th Street
New York, NY 10024
212-877-0229

HERMAN & LIPTON *
24 West 25th Street
New York, NY 10010

STUART HOWARD ASSOCIATES
22 West 27th Street - 10th Floor
New York, NY 10001
212-725-7770

HUGHES MOSS CASTING LTD
1600 Broadway #705A
New York, NY 10019-7413

HYDE-HAMLET CASTING
Times Square Station
Box 884
New York, NY 10108-0218
718-783-9634

IMPOSSIBLE CASTING *
35 West 38th Street - 3rd Floor
New York, NY 10018
212-221-1980

KEE CASTING *
234 Fifth Avenue
New York, NY 10001
212-725-3775

JUDY KELLER CASTING *
140 West 22nd Street - 4th Floor
New York, NY 10011

KIPPERMAN CASTING INC. *
141 Fifth Avenue - 5th Floor
New York, NY 10010

LELAS TALENT CASTING *
P.O. Box 128
Guilford, CT 06437
212-875-7955

MIKE LEMON CASTING *
413 North 7th Street - #602
Philadelphia, PA 19123
215-627-8927
215-627-1574 Talent Hotline

LIZ LEWIS CASTING PARTNERS *
3 West 18th Street - 6th Floor
New York, NY 10011
212-645-1500

JOAN LYNN CASTING *
39 West 19th Street - 12th Floor
New York, NY 10011
212-675-5595

MTV ANIMATION *
1633 Broadway - 31st Floor
New York, NY 10019

MTV TALENT *
1515 Broadway - 25th Floor
New York, NY 10021
212-517-3737

MC CORKLE CASTING LTD *
264 West 40th Street - 9th Floor
New York, NY 10018
212-840-0992

ABIGAIL MC GRATH, INC. *
484 West 43rd Street - Suite 37-S
New York, NY 10036

BETH MELSKY *
928 Broadway
New York, NY 10010
212-505-5000

ELISSA MYERS CASTING *
333 West 85th Street, #1008
New York, NY 10019

NICKELEODON *
1515 Broadway - 38th Floor
New York, NY 10038

ORPHEUS GROUP
1600 Broadway - #410
New York, NY 10019
212-957-8760

THE PHILADELPHIA CASTING CO.
128 Chestnut Street - #403
Philadelphia, PA 19106
215-592-7577 Actors Hotline

LAURA RICHKIN CASTING
33 Douglas Street - Suite #1
Brooklyn, NY 11231
718-802-9628

TONI ROBERTS CASTING LTD *
150 Fifth Avenue - Suite 309
New York, NY 10011

CHARLES ROSEN CASTING INC. *
140 West 22nd Street - 4th Floor
New York, NY 10011

JUDY ROSENSTEEL CASTING *
43 West 68th Street
New York, NY 10023

PAUL RUSSELL CASTING *
939 8th Avenue - Room 301
New York, NY 10019

CAROLINE SINCLAIR CASTING *
NEW YORK PERFORMANCE
WORKS 85 West Broadway
New York, NY 10007
212-566-0255

WINSOME SINCLAIR&
ASSOCIATES*
314 West 53rd Street - Suite 106
New York, NY 10019
212-397-1537

IRENE STOCKTON CASTING *
261 Broadway - Suite 2B
New York, NY 10007
212-964-9445

STRICKMAN-RIPPS, INC. *
65 North Moore Street - Suite 3A
New York, NY 10013
212-966-3211

HELYN TAYLOR CASTING *
140 West 58th Street
New York, NY 10019

VH1 *
1633 Broadway - 5th Floor
New York, NY 10019

MARJI CAMNER WOLLIN &
ASSOCIATES *
233 East 69th Street
New York, NY 10021
212-472-2528

WORLD CASTING *
216 Crown Street - 5th Floor
New Haven, CT 08510
203-781-3427

YOUNG & RUBICAM
285 Madison Ave.
New York, NY 10017

California Casting Directors

The following casting director's are in Los Angeles & vicinity. Please don't phone or visit if indicated by *. Note: photos & resumes will not be returned.

ABC TELEVISION
2040 Avenue of the Stars
5th Floor
Los Angeles, CA 90067
310-557-7777

RACHEL ABROMS, CSA
606 N. Larchmont Blvd. # 4B
Los Angeles, CA 90004
(323) 931-4381

JOHN A. AIELLO CASTING, CSA
6250 Canoga Avenue
Woodland Hills, CA 91604
818-615-2148

AMERIFLM CASTING
375 West Broadway #3R
New York, NY 10012
212-334-3382

DONNA ANDERSON, CSA
606 N. Larchmont Blvd. # 4B
Los Angeles, CA 90004
(323) 931-4381

DEBORAH AQUILA *
Castle Rock Entertainment
335 North Maple Drive
Suite 165
Beverly Hills, CA 90210
310-888-3581

MAUREEN ARATA, CSA
606 N. Larchmont Blvd. # 4B
Los Angeles, CA 90004
(323) 931-4381

ARTIZ/COHEN CASTING, CSA
5225 Wilshire Boulevard #624
Los Angeles, CA 90036
323-938-1043

ASG CASTING *
12716 Riverside Drive
North Hollywood, CA 91607
(818) 762-0200

JULIE ASHTON
10850 Wilshire Blvd.- Suite 1010
Los Angeles, CA 90024
(310) 474-6308

HYMSON-AYER CASTING
100 Universal City Plaza
Building 5166 - 1st Floor
Universal City, CA 91608

PATRICK BACA, CSA *
8306 Wilshire Blvd., 7004
Beverly Hills, CA 90211-2382
(310) 658-1008

PAMELA BACK, CSA
606 N. Larchmont Blvd., 4B, Los
Angeles, CA 90004
(323) 931-4381

BAKER/NISBET
451 N. La Cienega Blvd.
Los Angeles, CA 90048
(310) 657-5687

RISE BARISH CASTING
21920 Lamplighter Lane
Malibu, CA 90265
(310) 456-9018

CAROL ELIZABETH BARLOW
Sunset/Gower Studios
1438 N. Gower St.- Bldg.20
PO Box 44
Los Angeles, CA 90028
(213) 993-7066

ANTHONY BARNAO
c/o The Profiler
7333 Radford Ave.
North Hollywood, CA 91605

DEBORAH BARYLSKI CASTING *
Walt Disney Studios
500 South Buena Vista St.
Casting Building 10
Burbank, CA 91521
(818) 560-3570

BCI CASTING
5546 Satsuma
North Hollywood, CA 91601
(818) 755-9235

LISA BEACH, CSA
606 North Larchmont Blvd. # 4B
Los Angeles, CA 90004
(323) 931-4381

THE JUDY BELSHE COMPANY
1010 North Lima
Burbank, CA 91505
E-mail: judybelshe@aol.com
562-434-0550

TERRY BERLAND CASTING *
Westside Casting Studios
2050 South Bundy Drive
Los Angeles, CA 90025
(310) 571-4141

CHEMIN BERNARD
Sunset/Gower Studios
1438 North Gower
Building 13 - Room 206
Los Angeles, CA 90028
323-468-4858

INA BERSTEIN/HILARY BOTCHIN
CASTING
PO Box 69453
West Hollywood, CA 90069
(310) 278-1981

BARBARA BERSELL *
1951 Pelham Ave.- #101
Los Angeles, CA 90025
(310) 470-1670

JUEL BESTROF, CSA
5225 Wilshire Boulevard - Suite 508
Los Angeles, CA 90036
323-934-8363

SHARON BIALY
PO Box 570308
Tarzana, CA 91356
818) 342-8630

BIG TICKET TELEVISION *
Sunset Gower Studios
1438 N. Gower, Bldg. 35
Los Angeles, CA 90028
(213) 860-7425

TAMMARA BILLIK CASTING *
Disney Studios
500 South Buena Vista St.
Building R-I
Burbank, CA 91521
(818)560-4087

SUSAN BLUESTEIN, CSA *
Sunset Gower Studios
1438 North Gower
Building 5 - Room 409
Los Angeles, CA 90028
(323) 468-3485

SUSAN BOOKER
PO Box 2223
Malibu, CA 90265
(310) 457-5537

LOREE BOOTH, TLC/Booth
6521 Homewood Avenue
Los Angeles, CA 90028
(323) 464-2788

RISA BRAMON GARCIA, CSA
606 N. Larchmont Blvd. #4B
Los Angeles, CA 90004
(323) 931-4381

EVE BRANDSTEIN CASTING
10880 Wilshire Boulevard
Suite 1200
Los Angeles, CA 90024
310-234-2200

MEGAN BRANMAN
Warner Brothers television
300 Television Plaza Blvd
Building 140
Burbank, CA 91505
818-954-7642

JACKIE BRISKEY, CSA *
4024 Radford Ave.
Admin. Bldg. Suite 280
Studio City, CA 91804
818-655-5601

BUCK/EDELMAN CASTING
4045 Radford Ave., Ste. B
Studio City, CA 91604
(818) 506-7328

BUENA VISTA MOTION PICTURE
GROUP *
500 South Buena Vista Street
Burbank, CA 91521
818-580-7510

JACKIE BURCH, CSA
12233 West Olympic Boulevard
Suite 170
Los Angeles, CA 90064

LIBERMAN/PATTON CASTING
4311 Wilshire Boulevard #606
Los Angeles, CA 90010
323-525-1381

REUBEN CANNON AND ASSOC. *
5275 Wilshire Blvd - Suite 526
Los Angeles, CA 90036
(323) 939-3190

ANNE CAPIZZI, CSA
100 Universal City Plaza
Building 2150 - Suite 8A
Universal City, CA 91608
818-777-1000

CATHI CARLTON
Westside Casting Studios
2050 South Bundy Drive
Los Angeles, CA 90025
310-820-9200

THOMAS CARNES, CARNES & CO. *
PO Box 4220
Los Angeles, CA 90078
(818) 377-3239

FERNE CASSEL, CSA
6566 Sunset Blvd., #306
Los Angeles, CA 90028
(213) 469-1925

ALICE CASSIDY, CSA *
606 No. Larchmont Blvd., 4B
Los Angeles, CA 90004
(323) 931-4381

THE CASTING COMPANY *
7461 Beverly Blvd., PH
Los Angeles, CA90036
(323) 938-0700

DENISE CHAMIAN, C.S.A. *
Warner Hollywood
1041 North Formosa
Writers Building #306
Los Angeles, CA 90046

LORI COBE - ROSS
2005 Palo Verde Avenue #306
Long Beach, CA 90815
562-938-9088

JOANNA COLBERT
100 Universal City Plaza
Building 2160 - Suite 8A
Universal City, CA 91608
(818) 777-7581

RUTH CONFORTE, C.S.A.
5800 Laurel Canyon Blvd. #168
North Hollywood, CA 91607
(818) 771-7287

CARA COSLOW
Carsey Werner, Director of Casting
CBS Studio Center
4024 Radford Avenue, Building 3
Studio City, CA 91604
818-655-6218

CRASH CASTING
COMMERCIALS
451 North LaCienega - Suite 12
Los Angeles, CA 90048
323-653-6537

CREATIVE EXTRAS CASTING *
2461 Santa Monica Boulevard #501
Santa Monica, CA 90404
310-395-8233
310-203-1459 Hotline

DIANE CRITTENDEN *
2321 Abbott Kinney Dr. # 200
Venice, CA 90291
(310) 827-7730

ANITA DANN
270 N. Cannon Dr. #No. 1147
Beverly Hills, CA 90210
(310) 278-7765

RICHARD DE LANCY
4741 Laurel Canyon Boulevard
Suite 100
North Hollywood, CA 91607
818-760-3110

LESLEE DENNIS
2400 Riverside Drive #100
Burbank, CA 91505
(818) 238-2203

ERIK DESANDO
2050 South Bundy Drive #200
Los Angeles, CA 90025
310-820-4033

ELINA DESANTOS
PO Box 1718,
Santa Monica, CA 90406
(310) 829-5958

DIC ENTERTAINMENT
303 North Glen Oaks Blvd. 4th fl.
Burbank, CA 91502
(818) 955-5632

DICK DINMAN, CSA
606 No. Larchmont Blvd., #4B
Los Angeles, CA 90004
(818)762-2733

DISNEY CHANNEL *
3800 West Alameda Avenue, Suite 529
Burbank, CA 91505
818-569-7500

DISNEY FEATURE ANIMATION
2100 Riverside Drive # 3445
Feature Animation Building
Burbank, CA 90004
(818) 560-8000

WALT DISNEY/TOUCHSTONE
500 South Buena Vista St.
Team Disney Building
Burbank, CA 91521
818-560-5151

DIVISEK CASTING, C.C.D.A.
6420 Wilshire Boulevard
Suite LL100
Los Angeles, CA 90048
323-655-7766

PAM DIXON MICKELSON, C.S.A.
Warner Brothers
4000 Warner Blvd., Bldg. 76
Burbank, CA 91522
(818) 954-3928

DONNA DOCKSTADER
606 No. Larchmont Blvd., 4B
Los Angeles, CA 90004
(323) 931-4381

CHRISTY DOOLEY *
CBS Television City
7800 Beverly Blvd., No. 3371
Los Angeles, CA 90036
323-575-4701

MARION DOUGHERTY
Warner Studios
4000 Warner Blvd.
Burbank, CA 91522
(818) 954-3021

DOWD/REUDY CASTING
The Casting Studios
5724 West Third, #508
Los Angeles, CA 90036
(323) 665-1776

MARY DOWNEY PRODUCTION
705 North Kenwood
Burbank, CA 91505
818-563-1200

DORIAN DUNAS, CSA
606 No. Larchmont Blvd., 4B
Los Angeles, CA 90004
(323) 931-4381

DREAMWORKS CASTING
100 Universal City Plaza
Building 10 - 27th Floor
Universal City, CA 91608
818-895-5000

NAN DUTTON, C.S.A.
3400 Riverside Drive
Suite 100
Burbank, CA 91521
818-238-2203

E! ENTERTAINENT TV *
5670 Wilshire Blvd., 2nd floor
Los Angeles, CA 90037
(213)954-2400

DONNA EKHOLDT
Sunset Gower Studios
1438 N. Gower, Bldg. 35
Los Angeles, CA 90028
(213) 860-7425

PENNY ELLERS
6345 Balboa Boulevard
Suite 220
Encino, CA 91316
818-757-7000

ENTERTAINMENT CASTING CO.
80 North Wood Road
Camarillo, CA 93010
805-383-6763

RACHELLE FARBERMAN
13601 Ventura Blvd., #686
Sherman Oaks, CA 91423
(818) 905-1805

LESLEE FELDMAN
100 Universal City Plaza
Building 10 - 27th Floor
Universal City, CA 91608
818-895-5000

MIKE FENTON & ASSOC.
14724 Ventura Blvd., Ste. 510
Sherman Oaks, CA 91403
(818) 501-0177

FLORENCE FIGUEROA
Una Chica Entertainment
PO Box 3863
Beverly Hills, CA 90212
(310) 205-2665

MALI FINN CASTING
303 North Sweetzer
Los Angeles, CA 90048
323-782-8744

MEGAN FOLEY COMMERCIAL
CASTING
Riverside Studios
12716 Riverside Drive
North Hollywood, CA 91607
818-755-9455

DONAVAN-FOLEY THEATRICAL
CASTING
12716 Riverside Drive
North Hollywood, CA 91607
(818) 985-9902

EDDIE FOY III
Dick Clark Productions,
2920 West Olive Ave. #108
Burbank, CA 91510
(818)841-6287

NANCY FOY, CSA
Churchill Studios
12210 Nebraska Ave. #57
Los Angeles, CA 90025
310-826-7801

LAURA FRANCIS
1801 Ave. of the Stars #. 240
Los Angeles, CA 90067
(310) 286-7208

LINDA FRANCIS
8833 Sunset Boulevard #202
West Hollywood, CA 90069
310-289-5974

CARRIE FRAZIER, CSA
606 No. Larchmont Blvd., 4B
Los Angeles, CA 90004
310-201-9537

JEAN SARAH FROST, CSA
606 No. Larchmont Blvd., 4B
Los Angeles, CA 90004
323-463-1925

DENNIS GALLEGOS CASTING
639 N. Larchmont Blvd.,#207
Los Angeles, CA 90004
(323) 469-3577

CASTING BY JEFF GERRARD
4420 Lankershim Boulevard
North Hollywood, CA 91602
818-752-7100

DAVID GIELLA, C.S.A.
12711 Ventura Blvd., Suite. 170
Studio City, CA 91604
(818) 508-3361

JANET GILMORE
Raleigh Manhattan Beach Studios
1600 Rosecrans Ave.
Building 4-8, 1st Floor
Manhattan Beach, CA 90266
310-727-2290

GLEASON/JASON CASTING *
15030 Ventura Blvd. # 747
Sherman Oaks, CA 91403
(818) 906-9767

DANNY GOLDMAN AND ASSOC.
1006 North. Cole Ave.
Los Angeles, CA 90038
(323) 463-1600

LOUIS GOLDSTEIN
PO Box 691037
West Hollywood, CA 90069
(310) 724-8969

GOODMAN/EDELMAN
CASTING
9157 Sunset Boulevard - #200
Los Angeles, CA 90069
310-724-8969

CHRISTOPHER GORMAN, CSA
606 No. Larchmont Blvd., 4B
Los Angeles, CA 90004
323-463-1925

MARILYN GRANAS
220 S. Palm Drive
Beverly Hills, CA 90212
(310) 278-3773

JEFF GREENBERG AND ASSOC.
Paramount Studios
5555 Melrose Ave.
Marx Brothers Bldg., #. 102
Los Angeles, CA 90038
(323) 956-4886

BARRIET GREENSPAN, CSA
606 No. Larchmont Blvd., 4B
Los Angeles, CA 90004
323-463-1925

MICHAEL GREER, CSA
15030 Wilshire Boulevard
Suite 777
Sherman Oaks, CA 92403

AARON GRIFFITH
8440 Santa Monica Blvd., #200
West. Hollywood, CA 90069
(323) 654-0033

AL GUARINO
2118 Wilshire Blvd., # 995
Santa Monica, CA 90403
(310) 829-6009

HBO
2049 Century Park East - 36th Floor
Los Angeles, CA 90067
310-201-9200

MILT HAMERMAN, CSA
606 No. Larchmont Blvd., 4B
Los Angeles, CA 90004

PHAEDRA HARRIS CASTING
2665 Main Street - Suite 200
Santa Monica, CA 90405
310-392-7424

SUSAN MARGARETTE-HAVINS,
C.C.D.A.
Chelsea Studios
11530 Ventura Boulevard
Studio City, CA 91604
818-762-1900

RENE HAYNES
1314 Scott Road
Burbank, CA 91504
818-842-0187

HENDERSON/ZUCKERMAN
CASTING
225 Santa Monica Blvd., Ste. 714
Santa Monica, CA 90401
(310) 656-3388

TORY HERALD
3100 West Burbank Blvd #101
Burbank, CA 91505
818-526-0909

HISPANIC TALENT CASTING OF
HOLLYWOOD
PO Box 46123
West Hollywood, CA 90046
(323) 934-6465

ALAN C. HOCHBERG CASTING
606 No. Larchmont Blvd., 4B
Los Angeles, CA 90004
323-463-1925

HOLLYWOOD PICTURES
500 S. Buena Vista St.
Team Disney Bldg., No. 212D
Burbank, CA 91521
(818) 560-2085

BETH HOLMES CASTING, C.C.D.A. *
Loudmouth Studios
13261 Moorpark Street
Sherman Oaks, CA 91423
818-501-5625

VICKTORIA HUFF, C.S.A.
5700 Wilshire Blvd
Suite 500 North
Los Angeles, CA 90038
323-634-1260

MIKE HUMPHREY
Westside Casting Studios,
12166 W. Olympic Blvd.
Los Angeles, CA 90064
(310) 820-9200

JULIE HUTCHINSON, C.S.A. *
20th Century Fox
10201 W. Pico Blvd.
Bldg. 12, No. 201
Los Angeles, CA 90035
(310) 369-1892

HYMSON-AYER CASTING, C.S.A.
100 Universal City Plaza
Bldg. 506, Suite. F
Universal City, CA 91608
(818) 777-6748

DONNA ISAACSON
20th Century Fox,
10201 W. Pico Blvd.
Bldg. 12, No. 201
Los Angeles, CA 90035
(310) 369-1824

STEVEN JACOBS, CSA
606 No. Larchmont Blvd., 4B
Los Angeles, CA 90004
323-463-1925

JUSTINE JACOBY,CSA
606 No. Larchmont Blvd., 4B
Los Angeles, CA 90004
323-463-1925

ALLISON JONES
Raleigh Studios
5300 Melrose Ave. - Flynt Trailer
Los Anjeles, CA 90038
323-960-4070

CARO JONES, C.S.A.
PO Box 3329
Los Angeles, CA 90078
(323) 664-0460

ELLIE KANNER CASTING
20th Century Fox
10201 W. Pico Blvd., Trailer 777
Los Angeles, CA 90035

CHRISTIAN KAPLAN
20th Century Fox
10201 W. Pico Blvd.
Bldg. 12, No. 201
Los Angeles, CA 90035
(310) 369-1883

DARLENE KAPLAN CASTING
11712 Moorpark Street
Suite 203
Studio City, CA 91604
(818) 509-0663

KELLY CASTING
Chelsea Studios
11503 Ventura Boulevard
Studio City, CA 91604
818-762-1900

KATE KENNEDY, KENNEDY
STUDIOS
10930 Ashton #410
Los Angeles, CA 90024
310-444-1488

BARBARA KING
14225 Ventura Blvd.
Ext. 32, 1st floor
Sherman Oaks, CA 91423
(818) 981-4950

AMY KLEIN, CSA *
606 No. Larchmont Blvd., 4B
 Los Angeles, CA 90004
323-463-1925

BETH KLEIN
Viacom
10880 Wilshire Blvd. # 1101
Los Angeles, CA 90024
(310) 234-5035

NANCY KLOPPER, CSA
606 No. Larchmont Blvd., 4B
Los Angeles, CA 90004
323-463-1925

EILEEN MACK KNIGHT
606 No. Larchmont Blvd., 4B
Los Angeles, CA 90004
323-463-1925

ROBYN KNOLL
225 Santa Monica Blvd., 7th floor
Santa Monica, CA 09401
(310) 394-4699

LARRY KOGAN
Mystique Films
5400 McConnell Ave.
Los Angeles, CA 90004
(310) 448-7182

ALLISON KOHLER, CSA
606 No. Larchmont Blvd., 4B
Los Angeles, CA 90004
323-463-1925

DOROTHY KOSTER CASTING *
Crystal Sky Productions
1901 Avenue of the Stars
Los Angeles, CA 90067
(310) 843-0223

ULRICH/DAWSON/KRITZER
CASTING
3151 Cahuenga Boulevard West
Suite 345
Los Angeles, CA 90008
323-845-1100

DEBROAH KURTZ
1345 Abbot Kinney Blvd. Suite E
Venice, CA 90291
(310) 452-6800

DONALD KUSHNER
11601 Wilshire Blvd.
21st Floor
Los Angeles, CA 90025
(310) 445-1111

LANDAU CASTING, C.C.D.A.
Fifth Street Studios
1216 5th Street
Santa Monica, CA 90401
310-458-1100

SHANA LANDSBURG, C.S.A.
14852 Ventura Boulevard #201
Sherman Oaks, CA 91413
(818) 981-4995

LAPADURA/HART CASTING
Columbia/Tristar
9596 Culver Boulevard
Meralta Building

ELIZABETH LARROQUETTE, CSA
606 No. Larchmont Blvd., 4B
Los Angeles, CA 90004
323-463-1925

BARBARA LAUREN-RYAN
The Casting Co-Op
5724 W. 3rd St., #508
Los Angeles, CA 90036
(213) 932-1113

SALLY LEAR, CSA
606 No. Larchmont Blvd., 4B
Los Angeles, CA 90004
323-463-1925

CAROL LEFKO
PO Box 84509
Los Angeles, CA 90073
(310) 888-0007

HEIDI LEVITT
7201 Melrose Avenue - #203
Los Angeles, CA 90046
323-525-0800

CAROL LEWIS, CSA
606 No. Larchmont Blvd., 4B
Los Angeles, CA 90004
323-463-1925

LIBERMAN/PATTON CASTING *
4311 Wilshire Blvd., #606
Los Angeles, CA 90010
(323) 525-1381

LIEN/COWAN CASTING, C.C.D.A.
7461 Beverly Blvd. #. 203
Los Angeles, CA 90036
(213) 937-0411

TRACY LILIENFELD
CBS Studio Center
4024 Radford Ave., Bungalow 1
Studio City, CA 91604
(818) 655-5652

ROBIN LIPPIN *
846 North Cahuenga Boulevard
Building D
Hollywood, CA 90038

MARCI LIROFF
PO Box 48498
Los Angeles, CA 90048
(323) 876-3900

LONDON/STROUD CASTING
9696 Culver Boulevard #101
Culver City, CA 90232
818-552-3510

BEVERLY LONG
Moorpark Studios,
11425 Moorpark St.
Studio City, CA 91602
(818) 754-6222

MOLLY LOPATA *
13731 Ventura Blvd., Suite A
Sherman Oaks, CA 91423
(818)788-0673

JUNIE LOWERY-JOHNSON
CASTING
20th Century Fox
10201 W. Pico Blvd.
Bochco Bldg., No. 232
Los Angeles, CA 90035
(310) 369-1296

LINDA LOWY, CSA
5225 Wilshire Boulevard
Suite 718
Los Angeles, CA 90038
323-634-0700

MARILYN MANDEL
PO Box 691044
West Hollywood, CA 90069
(310) 271-2527

SHEILA MANNING
508 South San Vincente Blvd.
Los Angeles, CA 90048
(323) 852-1046

JACKIE MARGEY, CSA
606 No. Larchmont Blvd., 4B
Los Angeles, CA 90004
323-483-1925

KAREN & MARY MARGIOTTA
8060 Melrose Ave. #400
West Hollywood, CA 90046
323-658-1115

MINDY MARIN, CASTING ARTISTS
609 Broadway
Santa Monica, CA 90401
(310) 395-1882

MARTIN CASTING
Chelsea Studios
11530 Ventura Blvd.
Studio City, CA 91604
310-395-1882

LIZ MARX, CSA
606 North Larchmont Blvd., 4B
Los Angeles, CA 90004
323-463-1925

WENDY MATHEWS
Fox Broadcasting Company
10201 W. Pico Blvd.
Executive Bldg. 88, No. 328
Los Angeles, CA 90035
(310) 369-3849

VALERIE McCAFFREY
New Line Cinema 825 North
San Vincente Blvd., 3rd Floor
West Hollywood, CA 90069
(310) 967-6750

HANK McCANN *
1045 Gayley Avenue - Suite 200
Los Angeles, CA 90024
310-443-9650

MEGAN McCONNELL *
Raleigh Manhattan Beach
1600 Rosencrans Ave.
Building 4-B, 1st Floor
Manhattan Beach, CA 90266
310-727-2250

SUSAN McCRAY
PO Box 951
Malibu, Ca 90265
(310) 317-4400

VIVIAN McRAE
PO Box 1351
Burbank, CA 91507
(818) 848-9590

McSHARRY/WARSHAW CASTING
3000 S. Robertson Blvd. # 245
Los Angeles, CA 90034
310-558-5047

TOM McSWEENEY CASTING
1990 Westwood Blvd.#115
Los Angeles, CA 90025
(310) 470-7706

JOAN MELLINI
8281 Melrose Ave. #201
West Hollywood, CA 90046
(323) 653-9240

PAT MELTON/BENS CASTING
3960 Ince Boulevard #103
Culver City, CA 90232
(310) 202-4992

SANDRA MERRILL CASTING,
C.C.D.A.
Crossroads of the World
6671 Sunset Boulevard
Building. 1509, # 101
Los Angeles, CA 90028
(323) 465-9898

ELLEN MEYER
301 N. Canon Drive #300
Beverly Hills, CA 90210
(310) 273-7773

MIDDLETON CASTING
Universal Studios
100 Universal City Plaza
Building 1360 # 100
Universal City, CA 91608
818-777-1978

LISA MILLER CASTING
1040 N. Las Palmas
Building 24
Los Angeles, CA 90038
323-860-8183

RICK MILLIKAN
20th Century Fox Studios
10201 West Pico Boulevard, Building 75
Los Angeles, CA 90035
(310) 369-2772

LISA MIONIE, CSA
606 No. Larchmont Blvd., 4B
Los Angeles, CA 90004
323-463-1925

MITCHELL AND RAY CASTING, CSA
606 No. Larchmont Blvd., 4B
Los Angeles, CA 90004
323-463-1925

RICK MONTGOMERYCASTING
2372 Veteran Avenue
Los Angeles, CA 90064
310-841-5969

MOSSBERG/ANTHONY
CASTING *
1440 South Sepulveda Blvd #394
Los Angeles, CA 90225
310-444-8370

HELEN MOSSLER
Paramount Studios
5555 Melrose Ave.
Bluhdom Bldg., Room 128
Los Angeles, CA 90038
(323) 956-5578

JOHN MULKEEN, CASTING
1728 Alvira Street
Los Angeles, CA 90035
323-938-6556

MTV NETWORK *
2600 Colorado Ave.
Santa Monica, CA 90404

ROGER MUSSENDEN, CSA
10536 Culver Blvd. - Suite C
Culver City, CA 90232
310-559-9334

NBC
3000 West Alameda Ave.
Burbank, CA 91523
818-840-4444

NANCY NAYOR CASTING, C.S.A.
6320 Commodore Sloat Drive
Los Angeles, CA 90048
323-857-0151

DEBRA NEATHERY
4820 N. Cleon Ave.
North Hollywood, CA 91601
(818) 506-5524

NICKELODEON *
2600 Colorado Avenue
2nd Floor
Santa Monica, CA 90404

NICOLAU CASTING
8910 Holly Place
Los Angeles, CA 90404
323-650-9899

MERYL O'LOUGLIN
7800 Beverly Blvd.
Suite 3304
Los Angeles, CA 90036
(213) 852-2803

OMEGA PICTURES
8760 Shoreham Drive
West Hollywood, CA 90069
(310) 855-0516

JESSICA OVERWISE *
17250 Sunset Blvd., # 304
Pacific Palisades, CA 90272
(310) 459-2686

PAGANO-MANWILLER CASTING
5410 Wilshire Boulevard
9th Floor
Los Angeles, CA 90036
818-954-7352

MARVIN PAIGE
PO Box 69964,
West Hollywood, CA 90069
(818) 760-3040

PANTONE CASTING
1662 Hillhurst Ave.
Los Angeles, CA 90027
323-953-1200

PARAMOUNT PICTURES
FEATURES CASTING
5555 Melrose Avenue
Bob Hope Building - Room 206
Hollywood, CA 90038
323-956-5444

JENNIFER J. PART
United Paramount Network
11900 Wilshire Blvd.
Los Angeles, CA 90025
(310) 575-7019

CAMI PATTON
4311 Wilshire Blvd., #606
Los Angeles, CA 90010
(323) 525-1381

PEMRICK/FRONK CASTING
14724 Ventura Boulevard
Penthouse Suite
Sherman Oaks, CA 91403
818-325-1289

BONNIE PIETILA
20th Century Fox Studios
10201 W. Pico Blvd., Trailer 730
Los Angeles, CA 90o35
(310) 369-3632

HOLLY POWELL, CSA
606 No. Larchmont Blvd., 4B
Los Angeles, CA 90004
(323) 463-1925

QUANTUM CASTING
3405 Cahuenga Blvd.,
West Los Angeles, CA 90068
(323) 874-4131

JOHANNA RAY AND ASSOCIATES
1022 Palm Ave., #.2
West Hollywood, CA 90069
(310) 652-2511

KAREN REA, CSA
606 No. Larchmont Blvd., 4B
Los Angeles, CA 90004
(323) 463-1925

ROBI REED AND ASSOCIATES *
1635 North Cahuenga Boulevard
5th Floor
Los Angeles, CA 90028
323-769-2455

JOE REICH, CSA
606 No. Larchmont Blvd., 4B
Los Angeles, CA 90004
(323) 465-3929

BARBARA REMSEN & ASSOCIATION
Raleigh Studios
650 North Bronson Ave. #124
Los Angeles, CA 90004
(323) 464-7968

GRETCHEN RENNELL, CSA
606 No. Larchmont Blvd., 4B
Los Angeles, CA 90004
(323) 463-1925

SHARI RHODES
1041 N. Formosa Avenue
Formosa Building, Room. 319
West Hollywood, CA 90004
(213) 850-2435

RODEO CASTING
7013 Willoughby Ave.
Los Angeles, CA 90038
(323) 969-9125

VICKI ROSENBERG CASTING
Sony Pictures
10282 West Washington Boulevard
Tracy Building #200
Culver City, CA 90232
310-202-3223

ELEANORE ROSS, CSA
606 No. Larchmont Blvd., 4B
Los Angeles, CA 90004
(323) 463-1925

RENEE ROUSSELOFF, CSA
606 No. Larchmont Blvd., 4B
Los Angeles, CA 90004
323-463-1925

DAVID RUBIN & ASSOC.
8721 Sunset Blvd, No. 208
West Hollywood, CA 90069
(310) 652-4441

DEBRA RUBINSTEIN CASTING
5700 Wilshire Boulevard # 475
Los Angeles, CA 90036
(213) 634-1220

GABRIELLE SCHARRY
Sessions West Studios
1418 Abbot Kinney Boulevard
Venice, CA 90291
(310) 471-7320

JEAN SCOCCIMARO
CRC Productions
8222 Melrose Ave. # 301
West Hollywood, CA 90046
(323) 658-7224

BRIEN SCOTT CSA, CCAA *
SGI Marketing
18034 Ventura Blvd., # 275
Encino, CA 91316
(818) 343-3669

SUSAN SCUDDER, CSA
606 No. Larchmont Blvd., 4B
Los Angeles, CA 90004
(323) 463-1925

EINA SEOLER
PO Box 46321
Los Angeles, CA 90046
(818) 382-7929

LILA SELIK CASTING *
1551 S. Robertson Blvd., # 202
Los Angeles, CA 90035
(310) 556-2444

FRANCENE SELKIRK
Shooting From The Hip Casting
Zydech Studios
11317 Ventura Boulevard
Studio City, CA 91604

SELZER/FREEMAN CASTING, CSA
1438 North Gower Street
Building 5 - Suite 301
Los Angeles, CA 90028
323-468-3215

PAMELA SHAE, V.P., TALENT
Spelling Television, Inc.,
5700 Wilshire Blvd., # 575
Los Angeles, CA 90036
(323) 965-5784

SHANER/TESTA CASTING, C.S.A.
3875 Wilshire Boulevard #700
Los Angeles, CA 90010
(213) 382-3375

BILL SHEPARD, CSA
606 No. Larchmont Blvd., 4B
Los Angeles, CA 90004
(323) 463-1925

AVA SHEVITT
Village Studio
519 Broadway
Santa Monica, CA 09401
(310) 656-4600

JENNIFER SHULL, CSA
606 No. Larchmont Blvd., 4B
Los Angeles, CA 90004
(323) 463-1925

MARCIA SHULMAN
20th Century Fox
Building 730
310-369-3405

MARK SIKES
Pioneer Valley Productions
8909 Olympic Boulevard #120
Los Angeles, CA 90211
310-652-9599

MARGERY SIMKIN, CSA
606 No. Larchmont Blvd., 4B
Los Angeles, CA 90004
(323) 463-1925

JOAN SIMMONS
4841 Fir Avenue
Seal Beach, CA 90740
(310) 430-7392

CLAIR SINNETT CASTING
427 Talbert Street
Playa Del Rey, CA 90293
310-574-9131

MELISSA SKOFF CASTING, C.S.A.
C/O Paramount Studios
5555 Melrose Avenue
Clara Bow Bldg. #223
Los Angeles, CA 90038
323-956-2544

SLATE, PLEASE
Film Industry Workshops
4047 Radford Ave.
Studio City, CA 916904
(818) 785-9568

SLATER/BROOKSBANK CASTING *
1000 North Steward Street
Los Angeles, CA 90038
323-860-0138

JANE SHANNON SMITH
Paramount Pictures,
5555 Melrose Ave.
Los Angeles, CA 09404
(323) 956-5480

SPELLING TELEVISION INC. *
5700 Wilshire Boulevard #575
Los Angeles, CA 90036
323-965-5784

20TH CENTURY FOX FEATURE
CASTING
10201 West Pico Blvd
Los Angeles, CA 90035
310-369-1000

TURNER NETWORK TELEVISION
1888 Century Park East - 14th Floor
Los Angeles, CA 90067
310-551-6300

TOUCHSTONE TELEVISION/ABC
Entertainment Television Group
2040 Avenue of the Stars - 5th Floor
Los Angeles, CA 90067
310-557-7313

UPN (UNITED PARAMOUNT
NETWORK)
11800 Wilshire Boulevard
Los Angeles, CA 90025
310-575-7000

UNIVERSAL STUDIOS
Feature Film & Television Casting
100 Universal City Plaza
Universal City, CA 91608
818-777-1000

The WB
3701 West Oak Street
Building 34-R, Room 161
Burbank, CA 91505
818-977-6016

WARNER BROTHERS FEATURE
FILM CASTING
4300 Warner Boulevard
Burbank, CA 91522
818-954-8000

WARNER BROTHERS TELEVISON
CASTING
300 Television plaza
Building 140 - 1st Floor
Burbank, CA 95105
818-954-7646

WEBER & ASSOCIATES CASTING
MGM *
2400 Broadway Avenue - Suite 340
Santa Monica, CA 90404
310-449-3685

New York Commercial Producers

These are company's that produce television commercials. Do not call or visit. Do not send photos and resumes unless indicated with an *.

ARF
710 Clinton Street
Hoboken, NJ 07030
201-963-5900

ARTISTS COMPANY/A&R GROUP
38 West 21st Street
New York, NY 10010
212-477-4200

ANDROZZI PRODUCTIONS
118 East 25th Street
New York, NY 10010
212-647-1300

CROSSROADS FILMS
136 West 21st Street
5th Floor
New York, NY 10011

DIGITAL ILLUSIONS STUDIOS *
103 Grand Avenue
Palisades Park, NJ 07650
201-944-3627

EUE / SCREEN GEMS LTD
222 East 44th Street
New York, NY 10017
212-867-4030

STEVE & LINDA HORN, INC.
435 East 83rd Street
New York, NY 10028
212-794-1300

IMAGE GROUP POST (MTI)
401 Fifth Avenue
New York, NY 10016
212-592-0600

IRIS FILMS
63 West 83rd Street
New York, NY 10024
212-721-6400

JC PRODUCTIONS
P.O Box 1851
Murray Hill Station, NY 10016
212-391-0093

RICK LEVINE PRODUCTIONS
8 West 19th Street
32nd Floor
New York, NY 10011
212-734-9600

LOVINGER/COHN & ASSOCIATES
172 Duane Street
New York, NY 10019
212-941-7900

MERCURY PRODUCTIONS
655 Avenue of the Americas
New York, NY 10019
212-366-5800

NO SOAP PRODUCTIONS
1600 Broadway - Suite 40⁻
New York, N⁻¹
212-581-55⁷

LEE ROTHBURG PRODUCTIONS *
3 Dag Hammerskjold Plaza
New York, NY 10017
212-759-0822

SUGGS MEDIA PRODUCTIONS *
60 Madison Ave. - Suite 101
New York, NY 10010
212-689-9047

VIDEOACTIVE PRODUCTIONS/
VOICEWORKS SOUND STUDIOS
353 West 48th Street - 2nd Floor
New York, NY 10036
212-541-6592

WINDSOR VIDEO
8 West 38th Street - 2nd Floor
New York, NY 10018
212-944-9090

New York Advertising Agencies

TV Casting Contacts & Procedures

Note: The following is a listing of some of the top advertising agencies in New York. The Casting Director is the person to whom you should direct your mail. All agencies listed specify that you DON'T PHONE or VISIT, a request that you should always respect.

N.W. AYER & PARTNERS
Worldwide Plaza
825 Eighth Avenue
New York, NY 10019-7498
212-474-5000

BATTON, BARTON, DURSTINE
& OSBORNE, INC.
1285 Avenue of the Americas
New York, NY 10019
212-459-5000

D'ARCY MASIUS BENTON &
BOWLES
1675 Broadway
New York, NY 10019

GREY ADVERTISING
777 Third Avenue
New York, NY 10017
212-546-2000

OGILVY & MAHER
309 West 49th Street
New York, NY 10014
212-237-4000

SAATCHI & SAATCHI
ADVERTISING
375 Hudson Street
New York, NY 10014

YOUNG & RUBICAM, INC.
285 Madison Avenue
New York, NY 10017
212-210-3000

Network Program Packagers - Live & Film

The following is a list of companies that produce for network and cable television.

ABC PRODUCTIONS
2020 Avenue of the Stars, 5th Floor
Los Angeles, CA 90067
310-557-6800

ALLIANCE ATLANTIS
COMMUNICATIONS
121 Bloor Street East #800
Toronto, Ontario M4W3M5
416-967-1174

8087 Wilshire Boulevard, 3rd Floor
Beverly Hills, CA 90210
818-967-1174

AXELROD/WIDDOES
PRODUCTIONS
100 Universal City Plaza
Building 447, Room 245
Universal City, CA 91608
818-866-0355

BALTIMORE/SPRING CREEK
4000 Warner Boulevard, Building 81
Burbank, CA 91522-0812
815-954-2666

BANKSTREET PICTURES
414 West 14th Street, 2nd Floor
New York, NY 10014
212-645-0717

BARWOOD FILMS
330 West 58th Street, Suite 301
New York, NY 10019
212-765-7191

BELLISARIUS PRODUCTIONS
C/O Paramount Studios
5555 Melrose Avenue
Clara Bow Building - #204
Hollywood, CA 90038
323-856-8560

THE BEDFORD FALLS GROUP
409 Santa Monica Boulevard
Santa Monica, CA 90401
212-395-3553

BELL-PHILLIPS TV PRODUCTIONS
7800 Beverly Boulevard, Suite 3371
Los Angeles, CA
323-575-4138

BIG TICKET TELEVISION
C/O Sunset Gower Studios
1438 North Gower
Building 35, Box 45
Los Angeles, CA 90028
323-850-7400

STEVEN BOCHCO PRODUCTIONS
10201 West Pico Boulevard, Building 1
Los Angeles, CA 90035
310-369-2400

BRIGHT-KAUFFMAN-CRANE
PRODUCTIONS
4000 Warner Boulevard
Building 160, Suite 750
Burbank, CA 91522
818-977-7777

BRILLSTEIN-GREY
ENTERTAINMENT
9150 Wilshire Boulevard, Suite 350
Beverly Hills, CA 90212
310-275-6135

BROADWAY VIDEO
1619 Broadway - 9th Floor
New York, NY 10019
212-265-7621

STEPHEN J. CANNELL
PRODUCTIONS
7083 Hollywood Boulevard
Los Angeles, CA 90028
213-465-5800

CBS PRODUCTIONS
7800 Beverly Boulevard
Los Angeles, CA 90036
323-575-2345

CAPITAL CITIES/ABC
ENTERTAINMENT
2040 Avenue of the Stars, 5th Floor
Los Angeles, CA 90067-4785
310-557-7777

CARSEY-WERNER COMPANY
4024 Radford Avenue, Building 3
Studio City, CA 91604
818-655-5598

CASTLE ROCK
ENTERTAINMENT
335 North Maple Drive, Suite 135
Beverly Hills, CA 90210
310-285-2300

DICK CLARK PRODUCTIONS
3003 West Olive Avenue
Burbank, CA 91505
818-841-7300

COLUMBIA PICTURES
9336 West Washington Boulevard
Culver City, CA 90235
310-244-4000

550 Madison Avenue
New York, NY 10022
212-833-8500

COSGROVE-MEURER
PRODUCTIONS
4303 West Verdugo Avenue
Burbank, CA 91505
818-843-5600

DIC ENTERTAINMENT, L.P.
303 North Glenoaks Boulevard
Burbank, CA 91502
818-955-5430

DREAMWORKS SKG
100 Universal City Plaza, Bungalow 477
Universal City, CA 91608
818-733-7000

EYEMARK ENTERTAINMENT
10877 Wilshire Boulevard, 9th Floor
Los Angeles, CA 90024
310-446-8000

THE FINNEGAN PINCHUK CO.
4225 Coldwater Canyon
Studio City, CA 91604
818-508-5814

FOUNTAINHEAD FILMS, INC.
33 West 17th Street
New York, NY 10011
212-620-0966

40 ACRES AND A MULE
124 Dekalb Avenue
Brooklyn, NY 11217
718-624-3703

8899 Beverly Boulevard, Suite 2221
Los Angeles, CA 90232
310-244-4222

GRACIE FILMS
10202 West Washington Boulevard
Sidney Poitier Building - Suite 2221
Los Angeles, CA 90232
310-244-4222

GRANVILLE PRODUCTIONS
1223 North 23rd Street
Washington, NC 28405
910-343-3550

THE GREENBLATT-JANOLLARI
STUDIO
9346 Civic Center
Beverly Hills, CA 90210
310-860-3608

MERV GRIFFIN PRODUCTIONS
9860 Wilshire Boulevard
Beverly Hills, CA 90210
310-859-0188

GREYSTONE COMMUNICATIONS
5161 Lankershim Boulevard, Suite 280
North Hollywood, CA 91601
818-762-2900

GROSSO JACOBSON
PRODUCTIONS
767 Third Avenue - 15th Floor
New York, NY 10017
212-644-6909

5757 Wilshire Boulevard, Penthouse 1
Los Angeles, CA 90036
323-634-8634

HARPO FILMS
345 North Maple Drive #315
Beverly Hills, CA 90210
310-278-5559

HARPO STUDIOS INC.
1058 West Washington
Chicago, IL 60607
312-633-1000

HBO INDEPENDENT
PRODUCTIONS
2049 Century Park East, 42nd Floor
Los Angeles, CA 90067
310-201-9300

HBO NYC PRODUCTIONS
1100 Avenue of the Americas
New York, NY 10036
212-512-1000

HEARST ENTERTAINMENT GROUP
1640 South Sepulveda Boulevard
4th Floor
Los Angeles, CA 90038
323-960-4096

235 East 45th Street
New York, NY 10017
212-455-4000

JIM HENSON PRODUCTIONS
5358 Melrose Avenue
West Building - 3rd Floor
Hollywood, CA 90038
323-960-4096

117 East 69th Street
New York, NY 10021
212-794-2400

IMAGINE ENTERTAINMENT
1925 Century Park East, 23rd Floor
Los Angeles, CA 90067
310-858-2000

JERSEY FILMS
10351 Santa Monica Boulevard
Suite 200
Los Angeles, CA 90025
310-203-1000

DAVID E. KELLEY PRODUCTIONS
10201 West Pico Boulevard
Building 80, Room 26
Los Angeles, CA 90035
310-369-3717

BRAD LACHMAN PRODUCTIONS
4450 Lakeside Drive #280
Burbank, CA 91505
818-954-0473

KUSHNER-LOCKE COMPANY
11601 Wilshire Boulevard, 21st Floor
Los Angels, CA 90025
310-445-1111

LANGLEY PRODUCTIONS
BARBOUR/LANGLEY
PRODUCTIONS
2225 Colorado Avenue
Santa Monica, CA 90404
310-449-5300

LUCASFILM LTD.
P.O. Box 2009
Santa Rafael, CA 94912
415-662-1800

MIRAMAX FILMS
375 Greenwich Street
New York, NY 10013
212-941-3800

7920 Sunset Boulevard, Suite 230
Los Angeles, CA 90048
323-951-2400

MUFFITT/LEE PRODUCTIONS
C/O Sunset Gower Studios
1438 North Gower Street
Building 35, Suite 250
Hollywood, CA 91522
323-463-6648

MTV NETWORKS
1515 Broadway
New York, NY 10036
212-258-8000

2600 Colorado Avenue
Santa Monica, CA 90404
310-752-8000

NEW REGENCY PRODUCTIONS
4000 Warner Boulevard, Building 66
Burbank, CA 91522
818-954-3044

PARAMOUNT
TELEVISION/PICTURES
5555 Melrose Avenue
Los Angeles, CA 90038
323-956-5000

1515 Broadway
New York, NY 10036
212-654-7000

PATCHETT KAUFMAN
ENTERTAINMENT
8621 Hayden Place
Culver City, CA 90232
310-838-7000

PEARSON TELEVISION
2700 Colorado Avenue, 5th Floor
Santa Monica, CA 90404
310-656-1100

PROPAGANDA FILMS
940 North Mansfield Avenue
Hollywood, CA 90038
323-482-6400

REPUBLIC ENTERTAINMENT
CORPORATION
5700 Wilshire Boulevard #500
Hollywood, CA 90038
323-462-6400

RYSHER ENTERTAINMENT
2401 Colorado Avenue
Hollywood, CA 90038
323-462-6400

SANDOLLAR TELEVISION
500 South Buena Vista Street
Animation Building 1E 17
Burbank, CA 90404
818-560-4250

GEORGE SCHLATTER
PRODUCTIONS
8321 Beverly Boulevard
Los Angeles, CA 90048
323-655-1400

SESAME WORKSHOP
1 Lincoln Plaza
New York, NY 10023
212-595-3456

HOWARD SHORE PRODUCTIONS
627 South Rampart Boulevard
Suite 323
Los Angeles, CA 90057
213-736-6665

FRED SILVERMAN COMPANY
12400 Wilshire Boulevard, Suite 920
Los Angeles, CA 90025
310-826-6050

SONY PICTURES ENTERTAINMENT
(TriStar Pictures)
10202 West Washington
Culver City, CA 90232
310-244-4000

550 Madison Avenue
New York, NY 10022
212-833-8500

SPELLING TELEVISION
5700 Wilshire Boulevard
Los Angeles, CA 90036
323-955-5700

STUDIOS USA NETWORK
8800 West Sunset Boulevard
West Hollywood, CA 90069
310-260-2300

TEN THIRTEEN PRODUCTIONS
P.O. Box 900
Beverly Hills, CA 90213
310-369-1130

TOUCHSTONE TELEVISION
500 South Buena Vista Street
Burbank, CA 91521
818-560-1000

TRI-CROWN PRODUCTIONS
3900 Alameda Avenue, Suite 700
Burbank, CA 91505
818-955-7337

TRILOGY ENTERTAINMENT GROUP
2401 Colorado Avenue - Suite 100
Santa Monica, CA 90404
310-443-3095

TRISTAR TELEVISION
9336 Washington Boulevard
Culver City, CA 90232
310-202-1234

20TH CENTURY FOX FILM
CORPORATION (TWENTIETH
TELEVISION)
10210 West Pico Boulevard
Los Angeles, CA 90035
310-369-1000

1211 Avenue of the Americas
16th Floor
New York, NY 10036
212-558-2400

UNIVERSAL TELEVISION
70 Universal City Plaza
Universal City, CA 91608
818-777-1000

445 Park Avenue
New York, NY 10022
212-331-2400

VIACOM PRODUCTIONS
10880 Wilshire Boulevard #1101
Los Angeles, CA 90024
310-234-5000

1515 Broadway
New York, NY 10036
212-258-8000

VIN DI BONA PRODUCTIONS
12233 West Olympic Boulevard
Suite 170
Los Angeles, CA 90232
310-442-5600

VON ZERNECK-SERTNER FILMS
12001 Ventura Place - Suite 400
Studio City, CA 91604
818-766-2610

WALT DISNEY COMPANY
(TOUCHSTONE TELEVISION)
500 South Buena Vista Street
Burbank, CA 91521
818-560-1000

WARNER BROTHERS PICTURES/
WARNER BROTHERS TELEVISION
4000 Warner Boulevard
Burbank, CA 91522
818-954-6000

75 Rockefeller Plaza
New York, NY 10019
212-636-5000

WIND DANCER PRODUCTION
GROUP
1040 North Las Palmas - Building #2
Hollywood, CA 90038
323-645-1200

WOLF FILMS
100 Universal City Plaza, Building 69-F
Universal City, CA 91608
818-777-1238

WITT-THOMAS PRODUCTIONS
1438 North Gower
Building 35 - 4th Floor
Hollywood, CA 90028
323-993-7000

Network Offices and Studios

All Prime-time programs are cast through individual offices as listed. Photos and resumes are accepted by mail only. DON'T PHONE OR VISIT.

ABC TELEVISION

New York Offices:
77 West 66th Street
New York, NY 10023
212-456-7777

New York Casting:
ABC
157 Columbus Avenue - 2nd Floor
New York, NY 10023
Rosalie Joseph, VP Casting

Los Angeles Offices:
2040 Avenue of the Stars
Los Angeles, CA 90067
310-557-7777

Los Angeles Casting:
Gene Blythe, Senior Director of Casting

CBS TELEVISION

New York Offices
51 West 52nd Street
New York, NY 10019
212-975-4321

New York Casting
Amy Herzig, VP of Primetime Casting

Los Angeles Offices
CBS Television City
7800 Beverly Boulevard
Los Angeles, CA 90036

Los Angeles Casting
Peter Golden, Sen. VP, Talent/Casting

FOX TELEVISION

New York Offices
1211 Avenue of the Americas
New York, NY 10036
212-556-2400

New York Casting
Meg Simon, Executive Director

Los Angeles Offices
10210 West Pico Boulevard
Los Angeles, CA 90035
310-369-1000

Los Angeles Casting
Bob Harbin, Sen VP, Talent/Casting

NBC TELEVISION

New York Offices
30 Rockefeller Plaza
New York, NY 10112
212-664-4444

New York Casting
Steven O'Neill, VP Casting

Los Angeles Offices
3000 West Alameda Avenue
Burbank, CA 91523
818-840-4444

Los Angeles Casting
Marc Hirschfield, Exec VP of Casting

UNITED PARAMOUNT NETWORK

New York Offices
445 Park Avenue - 6th Floor
New York, NY 10022
212-605-0665

New York Casting
No casting dept at this location

Los Angeles Offices
11800 Wilshire Boulevard
Los Angeles, CA 90025
310-575-7000

Los Angeles Casting
Judith Weiner, VP Talent & Castings

WARNER BROTHERS NETWORK

New York Offices
1325 Avenue of the Americas
New York, NY 10019

New York Casting
Jeff Bloch

Los Angeles Offices
4000 Warner Boulevard
Burbank, CA 91522
818-954-6000

Los Angeles Casting
Kathleen Letterie, Sen Exec VP, T & C

PAX

New York Offices
1330 Avenue of the Americas
32nd Floor
New York, NY 10019

New York Casting
No Casting at Above Address

Los Angeles Offices
10880 Wilshire Boulevard
Suite 1200
Los Angeles, CA 90024
310-234-2200

Los Angeles Casting
Eve Brandstein

Main Headquarters
Clearwater Park Road
West Palm Beach, FL 33401
561-659-4122

(No Casting at Above Address)

Los Angeles Dramatic Serials /Soap Operas

You may send your photos and resumes to the casting directors listed below. DON'T PHONE OR VISIT!

THE BOLD & THE BEAUTIFUL
CBS Television City
7800 Beverly Boulevard
Los Angeles, CA 90036
213-852-4138
Casting: Christy Dooley

DAYS OF OUR LIVES
Columbia Pictures TV
NBC Studios 2 & 4
3000 West Almeda Ave.
Burbank, CA 91523
818-8404089
Casting: Fran Bascom

GENERAL HOSPITAL
ABC-TV
ABC Television Center
4151 Prospect Ave.
Los Angeles, CA 90027
310-557-7777
Casting: Mark Teachner

THE YOUNG & THE RESTLESS
Columbia Tristar TV
7809 Beverly Boulevard, Suite 3305
Los Angeles, CA 90036
213-852-2537
Casting: Meryl O'Loughlin

New York Dramatic Serials/Soap Operas

You may send your photos and resumes to the casting directors listed below. DON'T PHONE OR VISIT!

ALL MY CHILDREN
ABC-TV
320 West 66th Street
New York, NY 10021
Casting: Judy Blye Wilson

ANOTHER WORLD
NBC Studios/Another World
1268 East 14th Street
Brooklyn, NY 11230
Casting: Jimmy Bohr

AS THE WORLD TURNS
CBS-TV
524 West 57th Street
New York, NY 10019
Casting: Tom Albany

GUIDING LIGHT
CBS-TV-Studio
222 East 44th Street
New York, NY 10017
Casting: Glenn Daniels

ONE LIFE TO LIVE
ABC-TV
56 West 66th Street
New York, NY 10023
No Phone Calls Or Video Tapes
Casting: Sonia Nikoro

Television Production Facilities - Los Angeles

ABC TELEVISION CENTER
4151 Prospect Avenue
Los Angeles, CA 90027
310-557-7777

CBS TELEVISION CITY
7800 Beverly Boulevard
Los Angeles, CA 90036
323-575-2345

CBS TELEVISION CITY
7800 Beverly Boulevard
Los Angeles, CA 90036
323-575-2345

CBS STUDIO CENTER
4024 Radford Avenue
Studio Cit, CA 91604
818-655-5000

THE CULVER STUDIOS
9336 West Washington Boulevard
Culver City, CA 90230
310-369-1000

FOX BROADCASTING
COMPANY
10210 West Pico Boulevard
Los Angeles, CA 90035
310-369-1000

HOLLYWOOD CENTER STUDIOS
1040 North Las Palmas Avenue
Los Angeles, CA 90038
323-469-5000

KTLA STUDIOS
5800 Sunset Boulevard
Los Angeles, CA 90028
323-460-5500

NBC TELEVISION
3000 West Alameda Avenue
Burbank, CA 91523
818-840-4444

PARAMOUNT PICTURES CORP.
5555 Melrose Avenue
Los Angeles, CA 90038
323-956-5000

RALEIGH STUDIOS
650 North Bronson Avenue
Los Angeles, CA 90004
323-466-3111

RALEIGH MANHATTAN BEACH
STUDIOS
1600 Rosecrans Avenue
Manhattan Beach, CA 90236
323-466-3111

RRON MAR STUDIOS
846 Cahuenga Boulevard
Los Angeles, CA 90038
323-483-0808

SONY PICTURES ENTERTAINMENT
(Columbia Studios)
10202 West Washington Boulevard
Culver City, CA 90232
310-244-4000

SUNSET-GOWER STUDIOS, LTD.
1438 North Gower
Hollywood, CA 90028
323-467-1001

TWENTIETH CENTURY FOX
FILM CORP.
10201 West Pico Boulevard
Los Angeles, CA 90035
310-369-1000

UNIVERSAL CITY STUDIOS
100 Universal City Plaza
Universal City, CA 91608
818-777-1000

VALENCIA STUDIO WEST
26030 Avenue Hall
Valencia, CA 91355
805-257-8000

THE WALT DISNEY STUDIOS
(Touchstone)
500 Buena Vista
Burbank, CA 91505
818-560-1000

WARNER BROTHERS STUDIOS
4000 Warner Boulevard
Burbank, CA 91522
818-954-6000

Television Production Facilities - New York

KAUFMAN ASTORIA STUDIOS
34-12 36th Street
Astoria, NY 11106
718-392-5600

METROPOLITAN TELEVISON
STUDIOS
1443 Park Avenue
New York, NY 10029
212-722-5500

SCREEN GEMS STUDIOS, LTD
222 East 44th Street
New York, NY10017
212-867-4030

SILVERCUP STUDIOS
43-22 22nd Street
Long Island City, NY 11101
718-784-3390

SILVERCUP STUDIOS EAST
34-02 Starr Avenue
Long island City, NY 11101
718-786-2065

TODD-AO STUDIOS EAST
259 West 54th Street
New York, NY 10019
212-265-6225

TRIBECA FILM CENTER
375 Greenwich Street
New York, NY 10013
212-941-4000

Special Talent Groups

(Not Unions/Not Agencies)

If you have a special talent, these are agencies that you should contact for bookings

Antigravity, Inc.
(dancers, gymnasts, specialty performers)
484 West 43rd Street, Suite 461
New York, NY 10036
212-279-0790

Big Time Talent
(in-line skating, other extreme sports)
Chelsea Pier - Pier 62, Suite 301
New York, NY 10011
212-336-6450

Casting Society of America
1600 Broadway
New York, NY 10019-7413
212-333-4552

606 North Larchmont Boulevard
Los Angeles, CA 90004
213-463-1925

(Not an agency -do not send pictures)

Gospel Singers Now
557 East 93rd Street, Suite 1-R
Brooklyn, NY 11236
718-485-4580

Hispanic Organizations of Latin
Actors (HOLA)
250 West 65th Street
New York, NY 10023-6403
212-995-8286

League of Independent Stunt Players
P.O. Box 196
Madison Square Garden
New York, NY 10159
212-727-7021

Naomi's World Of Entertainment
(look-alikes & variety talent)
14 Rodman Place
New Hempstead, NY 10977
914-354-4911

National Associations of Talent Representatives (NATR)
C/O The Gage Group
315 West 57th Street #48
New York, NY 10019
212-262-5696

National Conference of Personal
Managers
1650 Broadway - Suite 705
New York, NY 10019
212-265-3366

New York Fight Ensemble (NYFE)
(choreographers, fighters for TV etc.)
P.O. Box 558
Ansonia Station, NY 10023
212-946-1361

On Location Education
(Certified teachers for TV, etc.)
175 West 92nd Street - Suite D
New York, NY 10025
212-222-2302

Police Actors Association
(authentic technical advisors, principal
actors & extras)
44 West 24th Street
New York, NY 10010
212-645-2500

Skateworks, L.L.C.
(in-line, ice & roller skaters)
20 Paragon Lane
Stamford, CT 06905
888-SKE-Works

Sign Language Talent
P.O. Box 20046
New York, NY 10011
212-631-1180

Tutoring for Children, LTD.
(Certified teachers for TV, etc.)
914-234-4470

Wonderman Productions
(Look-alikes & variety talent)
101 Harding Ave.
Long Beach, NY 11561
4516-431-9119

Television Talent Unions

AMERICAN FEDERATION OF
MUSICIANS (AFM)
1501 Broadway - Suite 600
New York, NY 10036
212-869-1330

AMERICAN FEDERATION OF
TELEVISON AND RADIO (AFTRA)
260 Madison Avenue
New York, NY 10016
212-532-0800

5757 Wilshire Boulevard
Los Angeles, CA 90036
213-936-8100

DIRECTORS GUILD OF
AMERICA, INC.
110 West 57th Street
New York, NY 10019
212-581-0370

7920 Sunset Boulevard
Los Angeles, CA 90046
310-289-2000

INTERNATIONAL PHOTO-
GRAPHERS OF THE MOTION
PICTURES INDUSTRIES
80 Eighth Avenue - 14th Floor
New York, NY 10010
212-647-7300

7715 Sunset Boulevard
Hollywood, CA 90046
213-876-0160

SOCIETY OF STAGE DIRECTORS
& CHOREOGRAPHERS
1501 Broadway - Suite 1701
New York, NY 10036

8489 West 3rd Street, Suite 10448
Los Angeles, CA 90048
212-391-1070

NATIONAL ASSOCIATION OF
BROADCAST EMPLOYEES AND
TECHNICIANS (NABET)
(Local 16)
1865 Broadway
New York, NY 10023 212-757-7191

Local 57
3210 West Burbank Boulevard, Suite D
Burbank, CA 91505
818-567-9935

SCREEN ACTORS GUILD (SAG)
1515 Broadway - 44th Floor
New York, NY 10036
212-944-1030

5757 Wilshire Boulevard
Hollywood, CA 90036
213-954-1600

UNITED SCENIC ARTISTS
16 West 61st Street - 11th Floor
New York, NY 10018
212-581-0300

5410 Wilshire Boulevard - #407
213-965-0957 Los Angeles, CA 90036

WRITERS GUILD OF AMERICA
559 West 57th Street
New York, NY 10019
212-767-7800

7000 West 3rd
Los Angeles, CA 90048
213-951-4000

Non Television Talent Unions

Four A's
165 West 46th Street
New York, NY 10036
212-869-0358

Actors Equity Association (AEA)
165 West 46th Street
New York, NY 10036
212-869-8530

6430 West Sunset Boulevard
Los Angeles, CA 90028
213-462-2334

American Guild of Musical Artists
(AGMA)
1727 Broadway
New York, NY 10019-5284
212-265-3687

Society of Stage Directors
1501 Broadway, 31st Floor
New York, NY 10036
212-391-1070

Theater Authority, Inc.
16 East 42nd Street, Suite 202
New York, NY 10017-6907
212-582-4215

Appendix C

Trade Publications

Audition News
6272 West North Ave.
Chicago, IL 60639
773-637-4695

Backstage
770 Broadway
New York, NY 10003
Phone: 646-654-5700

Billboard
770 Broadway
New York, NY 10003
Phone: 646-654-5400

Black Talent News
P.O. Box 83627
Los Angeles, CA 90083-0627
Phone: (310) 642-7658
Fax: (310) 642-7587

Daily Variety
475 Park Avenue South
New York, NY 10016-6901
Phone: 212-779-1100 /
Fax: 212-779-0025

Entertainment Weekly
1675 Broadway
New York, NY 10019-5820
Phone: 212-522-5681 /
Fax: 212-522-6104

Fashion & Print
C/O Peter Glenn Publishing
49 Riverside Ave.
Westport, CT 06880
888-332-6700

Film & Television
C/O Peter Glenn Publishing
49 Riverside Ave.
Westport, CT 06880
888-332-6700

Hollywood Reporter
770 Broadway
New York, NY 10003
Phone: 646-654-5500

Interview
575 Broadway
New York, NY 10012-3230
Phone: 212-941-2900 /
Fax: 212-941-2907

*Is Modeling For You? The Handbook &
Guide For the Young Aspiring Black Model*
c/o Amber Books
1334 East Chandler Boulevard,
Suite 5-D67
Phoenix, AZ 85048
Phone: 480-460-1660 /
Fax: 480-283-(

People
1271 Avenue of the Americas
New York, NY 10020-1300
Phone: 212-522-1212 /
212-522-0331

PerformInk
3223 North Sheffield, 3rd floor
Chicago, IL 60657
Phone: 773-296-4621

Premiere
P.O. Box 55393
Boulder, CO 80321
800-289-2489

Ross Reports
770 Broadway
New York, NY 10003
646-654-5746

Screen & Stage
C/O Peter Glenn Publishing
49 Riverside Ave.
Westport, CT 06880
888-332-6700

The Modeling Handbook
C/O Peter Glenn Publishing
49 Riverside Ave.
Westport, CT 06880
888-332-6700

The National Casting Guide
C/O Peter Glenn Publishing
49 Riverside Ave.
Westport, CT 06880
888-332-6700

Screen Magazine
16 W. Erie St.
Chicago, IL 60610
312-664-5236

Teen People
Time Life Building
Rockefeller Center
New York, NY 10026
800-284-0200

The New Yorker
20 West 43rd Street
New York, NY 10036
212-840-3800

U.S. Magazine
1290 Avenue of the Americas
New York, NY 10104-0101
Phone: 212-484-1616 /
Fax: 212-767-8203

Variety
475 Park Avenue South
New York, NY 10016-6901
Phone: 212-779-1100 /
Fax: 212-779-0025

Appendix D

Industry Websites

Websites are an important source of information in today's world. Here are some important websites that can help you on your journey to success:

▼ The Academy of Television Arts & Sciences - www.emmys.org

▼ The Academy of Motion Picture Arts and Sciences - www.lightside.com/ampas

▼ Hollywood Actors Network - www.hollywoodnetwork.com/hn/acting/index.html

▼ Acting Workshop Online - www.execpc.com/blankda/acting2.html

▼ Actors Online - www.actorsonline.com

▼ AisleSay - www.escape.com/-theanet/AisleSay.html

▼ Casting Connection - http://members.aol.com/rlshelly/rshelly.htm

▼ Casting Guild - www.castingguild.com

▼ Celebrity Archives - http://geocities.com/Hollywood/set/1150/index.html

▼ Children's Theatre - http://pubweb.acns.nwu.edu/~vjs291/children.html

▼ Yahoo! Entertainment>Actors and Actresses – dir.Yahoo.com/entertainment/actors_and_actresses

▼ Internet Actors Network Webring – www.aj_lawson.com

▼ The Musicals Home Page - http://musicals.mit.edu/muscials/

▼ Screen Actors Guild – www.sag.com

▼ Steppenwolf Theatre Company - www.steppenwolf.org/

▼ Talent Finder – www.iam.com

▼ Theatre-Express Home Page - www.theater-express.com/

▼ TVI Actors Studio Home Page - www.tvistudios.com

▼ The Virtual Headbook - www.xmission.com/~wintrnx/virtual.html

▼ The National Endowment for the Arts - http://arts.endow.gov/

These websites can help you further your business and legal knowledge of the entertainment industry:

▼ Social Security On Line - www.ssa.gov/SSA_Home.html

▼ Social Security Administration - www.ssa.gov/

▼ U.S. Department of Health & Human Services - www.os.dhhs.gov/

▼ U.S. Department of Labor - www.dol.gov/

Appendix E
State Labor Offices

Alabama Department of Industrial
Relations
649 Monroe Street
Montgomery, AL 36131
334-353-3580

Alaska Labor Standards and Safety
Division
Department of Labor
3301 Eagle St. #301
Anchorage, AK 99510
907-465-4855

Arizona State Labor Department
800 West Washington St. #102
Phoenix, AZ 85005
602-542-4515

Arkansas Department of Labor
Labor Standards Division
1022 High Street
Little Rock, AR 72202
501-682-4500

California Division of Labor Standards
Enforcement
6150 Van Nuys Boulevard #100
Van Nuys, CA 91401
818-901-5312

Colorado Department of Labor &
Industry
Labor Standards Unit
1120 Lincoln Ave #1302
Denver, CO 80203-2140
303-572-2241

Connecticut Department of Labor
200 Folly Brook Building
Wethersfield, CT 06109
860-566-5160

Delaware
302-761-8020

District of Columbia Film Office
717-14th Street NW – 10th Floor
Washington, DC 20005
202-727-6608

Florida Division of Labor
Child Labor Section
2002 Old St. Augustine Road
Building E – Suite 45
Tallahassee, FL 32399-0663
904-488-3044

Georgia Department of Labor
Child Labor Unit
148 International Boulevard
Atlanta, GA 30303-1751
404-656-3177

Hawaii Dept of Labor and Industrial
Relations
Division of Labor
Honolulu, HI 96813
808-586-8778

Idaho Department Of Labor
317 Main Street
Boise, ID 83735-0600
208-334-6725

Illinois Department of Labor
Work Permit Office
1819 West Pershing Road
Chicago, IL 60609
312-793-2800

Indiana Bureau of Child Labor
1013 State Office Building
Indianapolis, IN 46204
317-232-2675

Iowa Division of Labor
Child Labor Division
1000 East Grand Ave.
Des Moines, IA 50319
515-281-3606

Kansas Film Commission
700 SW Harrison St #1200
Topeka, KS 66603-3712
913-296-4927

Kentucky Film Commission
Capitol Plaza Tower, 22nd Floor
500 Mero Street
Frankfort, KY 40601
502-564-3456

Louisiana Department of Labor
PO Box 94094
Baton Rouge, LA 70804
504-342-3111

Maine Bureau of Labor Standards
Division of Minimum Wage and
Child Labor
Augusta, ME 04330
207-624-6410

Maryland Dept of Licensing &
Regulation
Division of Labor and Industry
501 St. Paul Place
Baltimore, MD 21203
301-333-4196

Massachusetts Division of Occupational
Safety
State Capitol
Boston, MA 02202
617-727-3452

Michigan Department of Labor
Bureau of Employment Standards
7150 Harris Drive
Lansing, MI 48909
517-322-1825

Minnesota Department of Labor *
Industry
443 Lafayette Road
St. Paul, MN 55101
612-296-2282

Mississippi Film Office
1200 Water Sillers Building
Jackson, MS 39205
601-359-3297

Missouri Dept of Labor & Industrial
Relations
Division of Labor Standards
3315 West Truman Boulevard
Jefferson City, MO 65102-0449
573-751-3403

Montana Department of Labor &
Industry
1805 Prospect Street
Helena, MT 59624
406-444-5600

Nebraska Department of Labor Safety
Division
State Office Building – 3rd Floor
1313 Farnum Street
Omaha, NE 68102
402-595-3095

Nevada Department of Labor
Capitol Complex
Carson City, NV 89710
702-687-4850

New Hampshire Department of Labor
Manchester, NH 03101
603-271-3176

New Jersey Department of Labor
Division of Workplace Standards
Office of Wages and Hour Compliance
Trenton, NJ 08625
609-292-2337

New Mexico State Labor & Industrial
Commission
1596 Pacheco Street
Santa Fe, NM 87501
505-827-6875

Human Resources Administration
Department of Social Services
Special Services for Children
80 Lafayette Street
New York, NY 10013
718-291-1900

North Carolina Department of Labor
Labor Building
4 West Edenton Street
Raleigh, NC 27611
919-733-2152

North Dakota Department of Labor
600 East Boulevard, 6th Floor
Bismark, ND 58505
701-328-2660

Ohio Department of Industrial Relations
Columbus, OH 43215
614-644-2239

Oklahoma Department of Labor
4001 North Lincoln Boulevard
Oklahoma City, OK 73105-5212
405-528-1500

Oregon Department of Labor and
Industries
Wage and Hour Division
800 NE Oregon Street #32
Portland, OR 97232
503-731-4074

Pennsylvania Department of Labor
Standards
1305 Labor and Industry Boulevard
Harrisburg, PA 17120
717-787-4670

Rhode Island Department of Labor
Codes Section
220 Elmwood Ave
Providence, RI 02907
401-457-1800

South Carolina Department of Labor
3600 Forest Drive
Columbia, SC 29211-1329
803-896-4300

South Dakota Department of Labor
Pierre, SD 57501
605-773-3681

Tennessee Department of Labor
501 Union Building
Nashville, TN 37219
615-741-2582

Texas Department of Labor Standards
Austin, TX 78767
512-794-1180

Utah Industrial Commission
160 East 300 South
Salt Lake City, UT 84110
801-530-6801

Vermont Department of Labor and
Industry
Wage and Hour Division
120 State Street
Montpelier, VT 05602
802-828-2157

Virginia Department of Labor and
Industry
Division of State Labor Law
Administration
13 South 13th Street
Richmond, VA 23219
804-786-2386

Washington Department of Labor and
Industries
Supervisor of Employment Standards
General Administration Building
Olympia, WA 98504
360-902-5316

West Virginia Department of Labor
1800 Washington Street East
Charleston, WV 25304
304-558-7890

Wisconsin Department of Labor
Madison, WI 53707
608-266-6860

Wyoming Labor Commission
Cheyenne, WY 82002
307-777-7262

Glossary

A cappella	Singing with no musical accompaniment
Account Executive	An advertising agency representative who serves as the point person between his or her office and the sponsor during the making of a commercial.
Ad Lib	Dialogue or physical action improvised by a performer.
AEA	Actor's Equity Association or "Equity" as it is commonly known.
AFTRA	American Federation of Television and Radio Artists.
AFL-CIO	The American Federation of Labor and Congress of Industrial Organizations. This is the parent body of American labor unions.
Agent	A company that is hired by an actor to represent them, and obtain jobs in the industry.
AGMA	The American Guild of Musical Artists.
AGVA	The American Guild of Variety Artists.
Air Date	The date on which a show or commercial is broadcast.
Audition	A performance in which an actor is evaluated for a role. Also known as a "tryout" or "call".

Avail

A situation in which an actor makes himself available to a producer even when there is no contract between them.

Background

Extras

Best Boy

Assistant to the electrician on a film set.

Billing

The size and placement of credits in advertisements for a theatrical, film, or video production.

Bio

A short biography or resume

Blocking

The planning of cast and camera positions and movements during a given scene in theatre, film, or video.

Book, Booking

When an actor/actress is hired for a job or assignment.

Boom

An extended pole to which an overhead microphone is attached. A camera boom is a crane used to extend the camera.

Breakaway

A prop or set piece that is built so that it breaks easily or can shatter harmlessly.

Breakdown

A cast list with brief descriptions of each role, used for casting purposes.

Business Manager

An expert in managing financial and tax-related matters for others.

Call

An interview with a casting agency, client or producer.

Call back

A second audition or interview.

Casting Agency   Agency that is contracted to audition, interview, or choose actors for a project commercial or advertisement.

Casting Notice   Posted information about an upcoming audition, as printed in a trade paper or placed on a union bulletin board.

Cattle Call   Slang expression for an open call, when a large group of people arrive en masse to compete for one or more roles in a production.

Clio Award   The most prestigious prize in the field of television commercials.

Close-Up   Term denoting a right camera angle, usually head and shoulders. In the script it may appear as CU.

Cold Reading   When an actor auditions with a script he or she has never seen.

Commissary   The cafeteria located on a motion picture studio lot.

Commission   The percentage of money that a performer pays to an agent or manager for representation.

Composite   An 8x10 photograph with several different poses of the actor.

The Coogan Law   A law established in California to protect the money earned by child actors.

Contact Sheet

An 8x10 proof sheet of all pictures taken in a session. Your contact sheet is what you will use to choose or pick the final photographs for your composite.

Credits

A compilation of one's professional and amateur experience.

Cue Cards

Cards with the performers lines written on them.

Day Player

A performer hired for a single day's work.

Demo

A short audio or videotape made for the purposes of submission to be evaluated by producers or managers for work.

Director

The person in charge of directing a production or project.

Double

A person who takes the place of another performer in a scene for various reasons.

Dresser

The person who oversees cast costumes and helps performers make changes of wardrobe.

Dubbing

Recording sound to match the picture after principal photography.

Emancipated

The age a minor can be declared an adult by the courts.

Exclusivity

A contractual condition by which a producer or advertiser has sole rights to a performer's work for an agreed period of time.

Extra

You are an "extra" if you are hired to play a silent role, or background character.

Fitting	A session in which one's wardrobe is tried on.
First Look or Look See	When the casting director takes his first look at an actor for an audition.
Franchised Agent/ Agency	This term is used to describe an agency that is registered with the Screen Actors Guild also known as SAG.
FX	Special effects such as explosions or physical tricks used during filming or taping.
Gaffer	A person who places lighting devices on a film set.
Glossy	A photo with a smooth, shiny finish.
Gofer	On-set helper available to "go for" things (coffee and supplies) or help in other ways.
Grip	One who moves set pieces or props on a film set.
Head Shot	A black and white photograph of the head and face or upper portion of the body.
Industrial	Film or tape used for educational or promotional purposes.
Interview	A meeting with a photographer, producer, director or casting director to evaluate you for a role before actual casting begins.
In the Can	A slang expression meaning the film is completed.
Lines	A script or dialogue that you have to memorize for your commercial or acting piece.

Lip Sync	To record a voice that matches the lip movements of the same or another performer.
Location	The filming or taping site when it is not on a soundstage or studio lot.
Long Shot	A camera angle that encompasses a broad scene.
Looping	The process of matching a voice to the lip movements of the same or another performer on camera.
Manager	A person that takes care of business matters for an actor.
Monologue	A pre-written piece of material equivalent to a short story or paragraph mostly used for acting and theatrical auditions.
Open Call	The session when a large group of actors is invited to be interviewed for a role. Open calls are posted in trades and on bulletin boards, and no appointment is necessary.
Out Time	The actual time a performer is permitted to leave a set or location and head home.
Per Diem	Money provided to performer on location to cover daily basic expenses.
Personal Manager	A person or firm hired to guide the career of a client by contacting and working with agents to set up auditions and interviews and offering a wide range of advice relative to career advancement.

Photo Double	A performer hired to perform on camera in place of another.
Portfolio	Usually an 11x14 zippered case containing one's photos and tear sheets of press reviews, ads and films in which that person has appeared. Also known as a "book".
Principal	The main performer in a television show, film, commercial, or play.
Producer	A person that finances a production or project.
Prop	Short for "property" referring to an object used in a scene.
Publicist/ Public Relations	A person or agency that handles publicity or the public relations aspect of one's career.
Reading	When an actor is called upon to act out a role while reading from the script, sometimes without benefit of rehearsal.
Release	A written agreement signed by a performer, which grants the employer certain specific rights.
Repertory	A theatrical company that presents several plays in one season, alternating them regularly every few days or weeks.
Representation	What your agent does when he secures jobs and auditions for you as his client.
Residual	A payment made to a performer for a repeat showing of a particular television show or commercial, or airing of a radio performance.

Resume	An actor's summary of their work history and other personal information. Resumes also contain stats that are pertinent to your acting career such as height, weight and hair and eye color.
Rights-To-Work-State	A state in which a performer is not required to belong to a union in order to work in any industry.
Running Part	A role that recurs in a television series.
SAG	Screen Actors Guild.
Scale	Minimum payment due for services under the various union contracts.
Scale +10	Minimum payment due plus 10 percent to cover the agent's commission.
SEG	Screen Extras Guild
Set	The actual locations where a commercial or production is being filmed.
Segue	In film or tape, a transition from one shot to another.
SFX	In scripts, refers to sound effects.
Sides	Also known as script, sides are the dialogue or words an actor will be saying for auditions, or jobs.
Silent Bit	A performance that requires specific action or "special business" without lines. An extra is frequently upgraded to a silent bit and earns extra money for it.

Slate	A small chalkboard and clapper device used to label the scene number, director, and production title to identify a given scene.
Sound Track	The audio portion of a film or tape production.
Stable	Slang term for a group of clients represented by a theatrical or model agency.
Stand-Ins	Extra players who take the place of principals prior to filming to help set lights and camera.
Storyboard	A rendering, frame by frame, of what a commercial (or other type of film) will look and sound like, usually in sketch form.
Submission	An agent makes a submission when he or she suggests a performer for a role.
Taft-Hartley Act	A federal law that states: 30 days after your jobs you will be required to join a union.
Teacher	The teacher hired by the studio to teach children working on sets.
Tear Sheet	A page from a newspaper or magazine showing an ad in which a person is featured and then used by the person as a sample of past work.
TelePrompter	The manufacturer's brand name for a crawl device that provides a performer with lines while looking directly into the camera.
Tight Shot	An extreme close-up.

Trade Shows	Productions by business or industry for the purpose of self promotion and product awareness.
Trades/Trade Publications	Publications that refer to the entertainment industry.
Turnaround	The number of hours between dismissal from the set on one day and call time for the next.
Type	A comparative term having to do with physical characteristics such as age, size, coloration and personal traits such as accent and ethnic background.
Understudy	The performer who rehearses and is ready to step in for another performer when he or she is indisposed.
Upgrade	Acknowledgment by a producer that a person hired as an extra has been given lines and performed as an actor and is thereby eligible for an actor's pay.
Work Permit	A document that is required by states that allows children to work.
Wrap	A slang word denoting the end of a production day or the conclusion of filming.

For more information regarding Chicago Sports &
Entertainment or Girl's Sports World, you can contact:

Kandias Conda
c/o Girls Sports World
P.O. Box 43575
Chicago, IL 60643
Phone: (877) 238-2551
email: GirlsSportsWorld@aol.com
email: CHGOSPORT@aol.com

ORDER FORM
WWW.AMBERBOOKS.COM
African-American Self Help and Career Books

Fax Orders: 480-283-0991
Telephone Orders: 480-460-1660
Online Orders: E-mail: Amberbk@aol.com

Postal Orders: Send Checks & Money Orders to:
Amber Books Publishing
1334 E. Chandler Blvd., Suite 5-D67
Phoenix, AZ 85048

Please send _____ copy/ies of *Get That Cutie in Commercials, Televisions, Films & Videos* by Kandias Conda.

Please send _____ copy/ies of *Wake Up and Smell the Dollars! Whose Inner City is This Anyway?* by Dorothy Pitman Hughes.

Please send _____ copy/ies of *How to Own and Operate Your Home Day Care Business Successfully Without Going Nuts!* by Dr. Terri Simmons.

Please send _____ copy/ies of *The African-American Woman's Guide to Successful Make-up and Skin Care* by Alfred Fornay.

Please send _____ copy/ies of *How to Play the Sports Recruiting Game and Get an Athletic Scholarship: The Handbook and Guide to Success for the African-American High School Student-Athlete* by Rodney J. McKissic.

Please send _____ copy/ies of *Is Modeling for You? The Handbook and Guide for the Young Aspiring Black Model* by Yvonne Rose and Tony Rose.

Name:_____

Company Name:_____

Address:_____

_____

City:_____State:____Zip:_____

Telephone: (_____) _____

E-mail:_____

For Bulk Rates Call: **480-460-1660**

ORDER NOW

Cutie in Commercials	$16.95
Wake Up & Smell the Dollars	$18.95
Home Day Care	$12.95
Successful Make-up	$14.95
Sports Recruiting:	$12.95
Modeling:	$14.95

❑ Check ❑ Money Order ❑ Cashiers Check
❑ Credit Card:
    ❑ MC ❑ Visa ❑ Amex ❑ Discover
CC#_____

Expiration Date:_____

Payable to:
    Amber Books
    1334 E. Chandler Blvd., Suite 5-D67
    Phoenix, AZ 85048

Shipping: $5.00 per book.
    Allow 7 days for delivery.

Sales Tax: Add 7.05% to books shipped to Arizona addresses.

Total enclosed: $_____

About the Author

Kandias Conda has worked with professional actors and entertainment professionals as an Entertainment Consultant. Her goal has been to bridge the gap between children and the entertainment industry. She formed an entertainment consultant firm, Chicago Sports and Entertainment, to provide unique and up-to-date information via books, guides, training sessions and mentor links, both in person and online. Ms. Conda's 12 year old daughter Demi originally began aspiring in the commercial industry, but embraced the music business much more fondly. She sings in her own singing group, naturally plays music by ear, sings in several choirs simultaneously, and has been cast in the leading role of many local plays and musicals. She has appeared in Cinderella and recently played Dorothy in the Wiz.

In addition to managing her daughter's entertainment career, Kandias has assisted singing and dance groups with opportunities to showcase their talent. Because Ms. Conda knew early that her daughter was destined for some type of entertainment career she launched an avid research of the entertainment industry, checking out every entity including commercials, acting and music.

Ms. Conda's research and symposiums have linked children and their parents directly with agents, music producers, professional actors/actresses, veteran children actors and their parents – all in an effort to give them a first hand look at the industry.